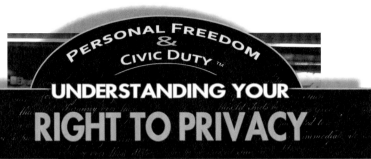

PERSONAL FREEDOM & CIVIC DUTY ™

UNDERSTANDING YOUR
RIGHT TO PRIVACY

KATHY FURGANG AND
FRANK GATTA

ROSEN
PUBLISHING®

New York

Published in 2012 by The Rosen Publishing Group, Inc.
29 East 21st Street, New York, NY 10010

Library of Congress Cataloging-in-Publication Data

Furgang, Kathy.
Understanding your right to privacy/Kathy Furgang, Frank Gatta.—1st ed.
    p. cm.—(Personal freedom and civic duty)
Includes bibliographical references and index.
ISBN 978-1-4488-4669-6 (library binding)
1. Privacy, right of—United States—Juvenile literature.
I. Gatta, Frank. II. Title.
JC596.2.U5F87 2012
323.44'80973—dc22

                                                    2010044139

Manufactured in the United States of America

CPSIA Compliance Information: Batch #S11YA: For further information, contact Rosen Publishing, New York, New York, at 1-800-237-9932.

On the cover: A New York City police officer searches the bag of a subway passenger. The police frequently conduct random searches of people's handbags, luggage, backpacks, and other personal items as typical security measures after the terrorist attacks on September 11, 2001.

CONTENTS

INTRODUCTION

Most teens today do not even remember the days when they could walk freely into an airport without having every bag scanned and sometimes inspected by authorities. They don't remember the days when they were allowed to keep their shoes on when walking through an airport checkpoint. Ask teens today about what happened to the right to privacy, and they might reply, "What privacy?" In a world where full body scans are permitted before someone gets on a plane, it is no wonder people are concerned with the issue of privacy rights.

Above: A Transportation Security Administration agent screens a passenger at an airport with a body scanner. Many security agencies rely on imaging technology to screen people instead of searching them by physical contact.

Stores and shopping malls are monitored by video cameras. School principals can ask that students be searched for drugs. Police can get permission to search people's homes. Cell phone towers can be used to reveal people's locations. Telephone conversations can be recorded, and records are kept of phone calls and e-mails around the globe. Are you ever really alone?

What is privacy, and what are Americans' rights to privacy? Louis D. Brandeis, associate justice of the Supreme Court, famously called the right to privacy "the right to be let alone."

But should people always want to be left alone? If no one is watching them, no one is protecting them either. The government may want to watch its citizens for their own protection. The government has the greatest power to invade a person's privacy because it controls the police and other law enforcement officials who can use force against its citizens. On the other hand, government force is also intended to protect citizens. Without some limits, though, people fear that the government could abuse the trust that is given to it by the voters. The right to privacy can be the only right that citizens have to protect themselves from government control. For instance, in the societies throughout the world where police are allowed to interfere with people's daily lives without restriction, those citizens live in constant fear of being watched. Ideally, the right to privacy protects people from having the government control areas of their lives that are important to their freedom and individuality.

Rights are entitlements that belong to everyone as a matter of law. Legal rights give people the ability to challenge the actions of others in a court. Rights can be given to people by a law passed by the state they live in, by Congress, or by the Constitution, which is the supreme law of the United States. Often, a law or a section of the Constitution is unclear, in which case a court must decide how to interpret important rights. In some cases, rights may conflict with one another. For example, if someone wants to write about your personal life, your right to privacy might conflict with that person's right to free speech.

The right to privacy first became an important issue in the twentieth century. The meaning of the word "privacy" is constantly changing. You will discover how the meaning of certain rights can change and grow. The idea of a new right may seem very strange, but you will understand that the law is always changing.

The right to privacy is unusual in that the word "privacy" is not ever mentioned in the U.S. Constitution. Nor is privacy ever mentioned in the Bill of Rights, which is a series of ten amendments that were the first to be added to the Constitution. The right to privacy is interesting because in some ways, it is nowhere but everywhere. Privacy is not mentioned in the Bill of Rights, but it is an important part of many of the other rights that are guaranteed in those constitutional amendments.

The issue of privacy rights has always been a complex one, and the events of September 11, 2001, made the world that much more complicated. Privacy rights had to be weighed against the importance of protecting Americans' lives from terrorist activity. Increased security at airports and in most public places was not questioned too much at first, but the more security measures were permanently put into place, the more people wondered when their privacy might return to "normal."

The USA PATRIOT Act of 2001 allowed more government surveillance and monitoring of average citizens than had ever been permitted before. The reasoning for the PATRIOT Act is that terrorists are living among Americans, which makes them a difficult enemy to detect and stop. Consequently, the government must be constantly vigilant and take every avenue necessary to catch those who are trying to threaten Americans' lives.

But with Americans' added protection came a certain loss of privacy. Today, it may be up to citizens to raise questions about whether or not their privacy rights are being violated. Knowledge about the law and the U.S. Constitution can help people know when to question the law.

THE ROOTS OF PRIVACY
IN AMERICA

Privacy is part of a culture. So as a culture's values change, ideas about privacy also change. The very idea of a private life is in many ways a modern concept.

THE EARLY DAYS

Many of the things that Americans take for granted as part of their private lives were not kept private two hundred and thirty years ago in colonial America. Colonial homes tended to be small, with few rooms and thin walls. Keeping conversations private was difficult because members of a family often slept and lived in the same room. Only toward the beginning of the eighteenth century was there more privacy in the home. In some ways, however, people had more privacy in the past—there were few newspapers or reporters, and solitude was easy to find because there were fewer cities.

Privacy was an important concern after the American Revolution. Many states demanded that some individual rights be guaranteed in the new Constitution before they were willing to endorse it. In response to these demands, the Bill of Rights was ratified in 1791. These amendments to the Constitution limited the power of the federal government (but not, at that time, the power of state governments) to take certain actions affecting people's rights. Although the right to privacy is not discussed in the Bill of Rights, many of the provisions of the Bill of Rights involve privacy issues. Privacy involves freedom from government intrusion into one's daily life, and the people who wrote the Constitution, sometimes called the Framers of the Constitution, were very concerned about these kinds of intrusions.

The Framers were particularly concerned with the right to privacy in one's own home. One of the most resented practices of the British troops stationed in the colonies before the Revolution was that of quartering. The Quartering Act of 1774 gave British troops the authority to force colonists to quarter them in their homes, providing them with food and lodging for free. The British could take over a person's house whenever they desired. In 1774, the British stationed their troops in Boston because they were concerned that the colonists were becoming disobedient. Bostonians severely resented having to quarter British troops, especially because they did not want them in their town in the first place.

The Third Amendment addresses this special concern about standing armies, or armies that are kept in peacetime, and the fear that people might have to feed and care for them during times when it is not really needed. This amendment was written because of the colonists' outrage against the practice of quartering, and some people call this amendment the Quartering Amendment. The Third Amendment says:

> No Soldier shall, in time of peace be quartered in any house, without the consent of the Owner, nor in time of war, but in a manner to be prescribed by law.

The Third Amendment has never been a real issue because there has never been a need for U.S. troops to be stationed in peoples' houses in their own country. But it shows that the Framers of the Constitution had very important privacy concerns in their day and were willing to be very specific to guarantee that those violations of privacy would never occur again in the new republic that they were creating.

The Fourth Amendment to the Constitution was also written to address intrusions into personal space. This amendment says:

> The right of the people to be secure in their persons, houses, papers, and effects, against unreasonable searches and seizures, shall not be violated, and no Warrants shall issue, but upon probable cause, supported by Oath or

In Texas, law enforcement agents inspect cars they suspect might contain cash or drugs and that are headed to Mexico. Officers can search cars without a warrant whenever the car has been validly stopped and they have probable cause to believe that it contains illegal goods.

affirmation, and particularly describing the place to be searched, and the persons or things to be seized.

The Fourth Amendment is about privacy in the home, but it is also about privacy from searches by officials like the police. Because of the Fourth Amendment, police must obtain a warrant before searching any person or person's home. A judge can issue the warrant only if there is "probable cause." And if the police obtain the warrant, they can search only for specific things. In addition, the courts have interpreted what it means for a search to be "unreasonable." For example, when police read someone his or her rights, they are following a rule that was established in the Supreme Court case of *Miranda v. Arizona* (1966), where the Court said that a reasonable search under the Fourth Amendment requires the person who is being searched to be told about his or her rights under the Constitution.

Another place in the Bill of Rights where people have located a right to privacy is the Ninth Amendment. The Ninth Amendment says:

The enumeration in the Constitution, of certain rights, shall not be construed to deny or disparage others retained by the people.

This means that people have other rights not specifically named in the Bill of Rights. Some believe that the right to privacy is or should be one of these unnamed rights that belong to the people. Other people believe that the Ninth Amendment is too vague. What does it mean to say that the people have many other rights? Some say that if Americans took the Ninth Amendment to heart, they could invent any right they chose and call it a right "retained by the people." The Framers of the Constitution simply wanted to ensure that naming specific rights in the Bill

THE FOURTEENTH AMENDMENT TODAY

The Fourteenth Amendment ensures due process and equal protection under the law to everyone. It also affirms that all people who are born or naturalized in the United States and subject to its jurisdiction are U.S. citizens. In 2009 and 2010, bills were introduced in the U.S. Congress that would deny U.S. citizenship to children whose parents are in the country illegally or on temporary visas. The question about who is really entitled to U.S. citizenship is frequently asked during disagreements over illegal immigration. There have been attempts to abolish birthright citizenship in Texas and California by state legislators, who want to bring the issue into the national spotlight and even challenge it before the U.S. Supreme Court, according to the Immigration Policy Center, based in Washington, D.C. Throughout U.S. history, with the exception of the *Dred Scott* decision by the Supreme Court, the Fourteenth Amendment has been the foundation of American civil rights. People who support birthright citizenship believe that all Americans would have a huge burden in proving their citizenship, and countless administrative systems would have to be created to grapple with the demands. What about the children born in the United States whose parents are refugees, or people who have sought political asylum? Would these children have no citizenship at all? Supporters of the Fourteenth Amendment also believe that eliminating birthright citizenship would be un-American, because birthright citizenship has been a part of American heritage since the birth of the nation.

of Rights did not exclude Americans from having other rights that were not named. They acknowledged that there were too many rights to name individually in the Bill of Rights, so the Ninth Amendment served as an umbrella that covered all of these "unnamed" rights. Over the years, privacy has become one of the more popular of those unnamed rights.

THE FOURTEENTH AMENDMENT AND CIVIL RIGHTS

The Bill of Rights applied only to the new federal government and not to the states. The federal government could not make unreasonable searches and seizures or quarter troops, but the states were restricted only by their own laws and constitutions. The states were worried about national, or federal, power and so they sought to preserve, not limit, their own power.

After the Civil War (1861–1865), the Fourteenth Amendment was passed. The Fourteenth Amendment guarantees equal protection under the law and due process for all citizens. Later, courts interpreted this guarantee as making the Bill of Rights a limit on the states, just as it originally limited the federal government.

Applying privacy rights against the states that were regularly abusing those rights was a hard-fought and important accomplishment. Many of the objectives of the abolitionist movement and later the civil rights movement were concerned with providing privacy rights that had been denied to blacks. The southern states did not respect the privacy of black slaves, since some did not even acknowledge that slaves were human. Southern judges said that blacks were not "persons," so they could not enjoy any of the protections of the law. Southern states passed laws called Black Codes, which severely restricted the activities of blacks. Slaves could not marry, own land, or earn wages; they could not testify in court against whites and could be punished with death for the most minor acts. Teaching a slave to read was classified as a crime. Slaves could never control their living conditions, and their lives were completely under the control of their owners. Therefore, slaves had no right to privacy because they had no rights at all.

Southern states, knowing the cruelty that they inflicted on black slaves, were afraid of slave revolts. They used a series of limits on the right to privacy to make sure that no revolts would occur. They went to great lengths to force northerners to return fugitive slaves who had fled to the North. Northern states would use police to search home after home to see if anyone was hiding fugitive slaves. These searches severely limited privacy of the home. The southern states searched the mail and read private letters for signs of abolitionist activity and regularly seized pamphlets promoting abolitionist views.

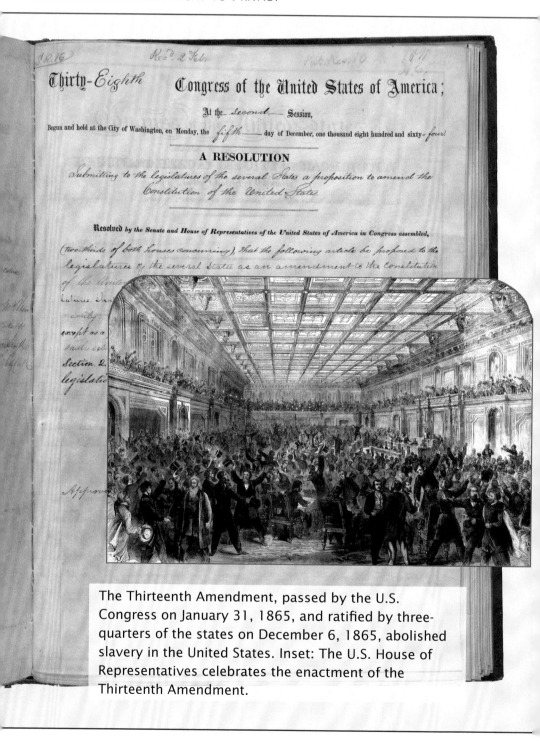

The Thirteenth Amendment, passed by the U.S. Congress on January 31, 1865, and ratified by three-quarters of the states on December 6, 1865, abolished slavery in the United States. Inset: The U.S. House of Representatives celebrates the enactment of the Thirteenth Amendment.

After the Civil War, in 1865, the northern states forced the former Confederate states to accept new amendments to the Constitution as a condition for rejoining the Union. The Thirteenth Amendment prohibited slavery, or involuntary servitude. The Fourteenth Amendment guaranteed equal protection under the law and due process to all persons born in the United States. This meant that, for the first time, the Fourth Amendment applied to the states as well as the federal government. And from that time, the states could not conduct unreasonable searches and seizures. The Fourteenth Amendment also says that the law must be applied equally. For example, if the police search only blacks, they are acting unreasonably and are not treating all citizens as equals.

The passing of the Fourteenth Amendment was a high watermark for civil rights, but the southern states soon eroded its power by enacting laws that restricted the freedom of the newly freed slaves, or freedmen. These laws were nicknamed Jim Crow, and they created a segregated society in which blacks were forced to be separated from whites in public and private places. Blacks could not ride in the same train cars, live in the same neighborhoods, go to the same schools, or eat at the same restaurants as whites. They could not marry whites, and grandfather clauses or unfair taxes and tests were used to prevent them from registering to vote.

When rights were denied, whether by the British or by southern whites, privacy rights were often the first to go. Privacy rights were denied to blacks as part of Jim Crow. By the 1880s, southerners had unleashed a campaign of violence designed to make blacks so afraid for their lives that they would not even try to gain full rights. Lynching occurred frequently—gangs of whites would form large mobs and publicly attack and kill blacks. Often the local police encouraged these white mobs. Very little privacy existed for blacks then, and if you were black, police could arrest you for sitting in the wrong place or for being seen with whites. The police were always watching to see if blacks crossed any of the lines that kept them in a subordinated position. Obviously, very little security can exist in someone's home if mobs can attack at any time and the police won't provide protection.

Real privacy and security for African Americans and other minorities have come slowly. Almost a hundred years after the Civil War, in 1964, a civil rights act was passed guaranteeing all people equal access to public accommodations such as restaurants, theaters, and buses. But as will be discussed in later sections of this book, problems with the police and with racism still exist. In their efforts to stop crimes from happening, police may harass or stop people just because of their race. In practice, privacy rights may still depend on what color a person is in many parts of America.

WHEN PRIVACY
BECOMES AN ISSUE

A lawyer named Louis D. Brandeis, who later became a Supreme Court justice, is thought to have coined the phrase "right to privacy." Although privacy is an important part of many of the constitutional amendments that make up the Bill of Rights, Brandeis was the first to argue that it should be a right on its own.

With his law partner Samuel D. Warren, Brandeis wrote an article in 1890 titled "The Right to Privacy" that later became famous. Brandeis and Warren complained in their article that the press was publishing too much information about people's personal affairs, and they put forth the idea that people should have the right to sue if their privacy has been interfered with. Brandeis wrote:

> Instantaneous photographs and newspaper enterprise have invaded the sacred precincts of private and domestic life; and numerous mechanical devices threaten to make good the prediction that what is whispered in the closet shall be proclaimed from the housetops. The press is over-

Actress Kristen Stewart, who gained fame in her role as Bella Swan in the *Twilight Saga*, is being pursued relentlessly by paparazzi. Many celebrities today complain that they have no privacy in their personal lives.

stepping in every direction the obvious bounds of propriety and decency. Gossip is no longer the resource of the idle and the vicious, but has become a trade.

This sounds like the complaints of today's celebrities and other public figures about cameras and tabloids following them everywhere. Advances in technology have made eavesdropping and taking photos of people in their private lives easier than ever before. Of course, people always lose some privacy if they choose to be in the spotlight. But how about the privacy of those who never wanted attention in the first place and simply want to be left alone? Brandeis argued that although the right to privacy was a new right, there was a basis for it in traditional law. He said that courts should recognize the right to privacy as a matter of common law. What does that mean? The oldest source of law in the United States is the common law, which is the law that Americans inherited from England. It originated in the time of William the Conqueror, and it was part of an effort by the king of England to make all citizens follow one law, or a common law. This English common law has always been a law of precedent, which means that judges must follow the decisions laid down in cases that have come before. The common law changes only when judges decide they must make a new rule to explain how a new case fits with the old decisions, or if after many years judges determine that the old rules are obsolete. The judges made common law very slowly over the years. Eventually, it developed into a large body of law. The American colonies adopted English common law as their own law when the United States won its independence because colonists were used to British laws. Adopting British laws was easier than trying to completely rewrite all of the laws on the books. Since that time, though, American judges have taken the old British rules and changed them. Brandeis believed that a right to privacy should be recognized as part of common law because it protected people from harm in the same way that many cases that had become part of common law already did.

Brandeis also recognized that the right to privacy has its limits, and he developed some of the themes that have become important in discussions of this right ever since. He said there should be a general right to privacy, but the government should be able to limit that right when it is in the public interest. He distinguished between a "legitimate concern" and an "unwarranted invasion" into people's private lives. However, it is very hard to draw the lines that decide what should be kept private and what is a strong enough public interest to justify limiting people's privacy.

Courts would gradually develop the idea that people have a right to privacy. In a 1902 case called *Robertson v. Rochester Folding Box Co.*, a flour company had used a picture of a pretty young girl on its flour boxes. The problem was that the picture was of a real girl, and the flour company had never asked for her permission to use the picture. She said that she was emotionally traumatized by having her image on all of those flour boxes and "greatly humiliated by the scoffs and jeers of persons who ha[d] recognized her face." She sued for damages to compensate her for her emotional distress. The court said that there was no such thing as a right to privacy and disparaged Brandeis's "clever article." Not only did the court not let a jury decide if the girl should receive any compensation, but it also said that she did not even have a right to sue in the first place. The legal term for a right to sue is "cause of action." The court said that she did not have a cause of action because no other court had ever recognized a right to privacy.

Many people were upset by the decision in *Robertson v. Rochester Folding Box Co.*, and the following year, the New York State Legislature passed a law saying that no one can use the name or image of a person without his or her permission. The New York law also created a cause of action so that if someone violates the law, the victim has the right to sue in court. This was the very first American law written to protect a right to privacy, and it was a state law. Federal laws, which apply to all of the states in the nation, would come much later. But by the 1920s and 1930s, this idea of a right to privacy began to take hold in several other states.

New laws and court decisions said that people could sue newspapers for publishing embarrassing private information, even if it were true. This was the very practice that Brandeis complained about in his article. This meant that the right to privacy conflicted with the First Amendment right to freedom of the press. Courts later began to limit the right to privacy to protect newspapers from being sued so often that they might become afraid to provide useful or important information to the public. Some cases bring up very complex ethical issues for a newspaper editor, who must decide how much information to include in a story.

When people think about privacy rights, they must balance private rights against the public interest. On the one hand, newspapers serve an important public purpose in reporting the news, even if it is scandalous. Newspapers, both print and online, inform the public and help people understand current events. On the other hand, some information might not have enough educational value or be newsworthy enough to justify the harm that it might cause to a person's reputation. Also, the possibility of discrimination becomes a concern if newspapers are allowed to selectively decide whose reputation matters less and whose matters more, or to otherwise infringe upon individuals' privacy in a biased manner. For example, should a newspaper be able to show footage of a person engaging in offensive behavior—for example, being drunk and disorderly in public? Or does such footage have no real newsworthy purpose and serve only to embarrass the person?

Newspapers are sometimes confronted with information about the sexual lives of politicians and sports figures. Should they hesitate to publicize stories about the marital infidelities of prominent figures? Does such information serve any socially valuable purpose? Is there any tasteful way to print or post such stories? Do public figures voluntarily surrender their right to privacy when they decide to put themselves into the spotlight to begin with?

Golfer Tiger Woods speaks to the media two months after he admitted marital infidelity. The media frenzy that surrounded Woods after his private problems became known prompted many people to wonder what purpose such scrutiny can possibly serve.

Many newspapers do not report the names of rape victims in order to protect their privacy and emotional well-being. Rape is so traumatic that many victims of this crime find it too difficult to even discuss. There is some concern that if newspapers could reveal the names of rape victims, many people would not report the crime to the police. Some states, including Florida, have passed laws requiring newspapers to keep the names of rape victims anonymous. However, the

SUPREME COURT JUSTICES

The U.S. Supreme Court makes some of the most important decisions that affect Americans. When a lawsuit cannot be settled satisfactorily in a lower court, the Supreme Court must often listen to both sides of the case and make a definitive call. Cases are decided by majority vote. As "court of last resort," the Supreme Court is the highest judicial body in the country, and the judges are among the most respected in the U.S. judicial system. The president of the United States nominates the chief justice and eight associate justices to the Court. Then the Senate questions the nominees. The nominees are asked to discuss their views on important and controversial subjects that may come before the Supreme Court. The Senate must consent to, or approve, the president's choice before an appointee can be on the bench. Justices serve on the Supreme Court for life. Only a conviction or impeachment can end a justice's life term. Otherwise, he or she serves on the Supreme Court until death, unless he or she wishes to retire or resign.

The U.S. Supreme Court gathered for a formal portrait in 2010. Chief Justice John G. Roberts is sitting in the center.

Supreme Court, in a 1989 case called the *Florida Star v. B. J. F.*, said that because it was the police department that gave the newspaper the information, and because the law only applied to small neighborhood newspapers, the law was invalid. However, the Supreme Court ruled to allow some limits on what kinds of information newspapers could publish.

These examples show how privacy rights generate controversy and how the courts have gone back and forth as they seek to define the appropriate balance between a newspaper company's right to free speech and an individual's right to privacy.

INVASIONS OF PRIVACY

By the late 1960s, courts began to realize that not only is the invasion of privacy very serious, but also that privacy can be violated even if nobody actually obtains any personal information. People can still feel that their privacy is being taken away if they are subjected to constant prying, or annoying (but failed) efforts to obtain personal information. Some courts have recognized that people should be able to sue if they are subjected to an especially severe intrusion into their privacy.

In one well-known case, Ralph Nader, a writer and advocate for consumer safety and former candidate for president, was targeted by General Motors (GM) after he began to speak out and question the safety of

GM cars, especially a Chevrolet car called the Corvair, which he argued was a deathtrap. He was about to publish a book about the Corvair, *Unsafe at Any Speed* (which would ultimately cause a national outcry over auto safety and become a best seller). GM was determined to stop Nader from publishing the book. The company hired private detectives to follow him in public, make harassing phone calls, and inquire into his private views and private life. Nader sued, and GM eventually paid him $425,000 to settle the case and denied any wrongdoing. In another troubling case, a doctor insisted on taking photographs of a dying patient. The patient objected by clenching his fist and shaking his head. The Supreme Judicial Court of Maine in *Estate of Berthiaume v. Pratt* (1976) decided that even though those photographs were never printed, the dead man's family could receive compensation because he had a right not to be photographed.

Privacy and Identity

People still sometimes sue when their images are used in advertisements, just like the girl on the flour box in 1902. In 2009, movie director Woody Allen sued American Apparel for using a picture of him in one of its billboard advertisements without his permission. The picture was of Allen in a scene from his 1977 comedy film *Annie Hall*, in which he is dressed in

דער הייליקער רבי

American Apparel

WILLIAMSBURG BRIDGE →

ALLEN ST

ONE WAY

TURNING VEHICLES

Actor and director Woody Allen sued the company American Apparel for using his image on a billboard in New York City without his permission. Allen won the lawsuit.

traditional Hasidic garb. He sued the clothing company for $10 million, but he later settled the suit for $5 million. Some people felt that American Apparel should not have had to ask for permission to use the picture in the ad because Allen is a public figure and his movies are a part of popular culture. But does this mean that the star has no right to privacy and can therefore expect to see his image used on a billboard without his permission? The issues of privacy rights affect all people, whether they are famous or not.

CHAPTER 3

PRIVACY AND LAW ENFORCEMENT

While a general right to privacy has been recognized only in a few areas related to family life, certain kinds of privacy are recognized in the Constitution. As stated earlier, the Fourth Amendment to the Constitution establishes a right to be safe from police activity that interferes with citizens' private lives. Police cannot enter people's homes without a warrant signed by a judge or engage in "unreasonable searches and seizures."

From early times, the right to privacy has been connected with having a right to be left alone by the authorities, especially the police. The police have so much power to interfere in citizens' private lives that it is especially important to limit their actions. And although the police have a great deal of power, the Constitution limits everything that they do in their daily work.

The Fourth Amendment prevents the police or other government agents from making an unreasonable search or seizure. The police must have a warrant signed by a judge and "probable cause" to make an arrest. They must have probable cause to believe that someone is engaging in, or about to engage in, a specific kind of criminal behavior. Probable cause is also described as having enough information to lead a reasonable person to believe that a crime has occurred.

Courts have said that if the police have a "reasonable suspicion" that someone is engaging in criminal activity, or is about to do so, they can "stop and frisk" that individual. For example, although the police may not have full probable cause to think that a man is about to shoot someone just because there is a bulge in his jacket, they might have a pretty reasonable suspicion that he is carrying a gun. They can pat him down to check for any concealed weapons, a process that is humiliating and that can also become violent. The police can conduct a full search if they discover a weapon in a frisk because they then have full probable cause.

In some situations, searches can even be performed with no suspicion at all, if and when important public safety issues are involved. Airline pilots and train operators can be given drug tests without any suspicion because so many lives depend on safe transportation. Do you think that random drug testing is justified by the concern over public safety?

Some state courts protect people against searches more than the Supreme Court does under the U.S. Constitution. For example, New York State requires

Officers of the New York City Police Department search a subway passenger's bag to thwart possible terrorist bombings. The police conduct tens of thousands of random bag searches annually. Any individual who refuses a search is turned away.

two more levels of suspicion, in addition to probable cause and reasonable suspicion. Most police departments are operated by a local, municipal, or city government, or by a county. A local police department may have its own rules and regulations regarding stops that are made. Sometimes, because of lawsuits, courts require police departments to follow a set of rules that protect a citizen's privacy more fully than the Constitution does when the police make stops.

BEING STOPPED BY THE POLICE

More and more young people are being stopped by the police and then treated as adult criminals instead of being processed within the juvenile justice system. In some rare cases, minors were actually given the death penalty. The Supreme Court ended that particular practice in 2005. But the sentences given to minors have definitely become harsher, and adult sentencing is being used more, even in juvenile courts.

If the police should ever stop you, it is important that you don't resist a search in any physical way. Resisting arrest is usually a crime. At most, state that you do not consent to the search, loudly and clearly, so that others nearby can hear you. Later on, you can make a complaint or take action against the police if they violate your rights, but do not try to vindicate your rights in person.

Do not run from the police. According to a 1999 Supreme Court case, *Whren v. United States*, running from the police can itself be grounds for suspicion and can lead to a police stop. Do not turn around because the officer might think you are reaching for a weapon. Stand perfectly still. Try not to panic. Stay relaxed.

Keep your hands in plain sight. Do not make any fast motions with your hands. People have been killed because officers thought that they were reaching for a gun. In a tense situation, especially at night, any movement could be mistaken for reaching for a gun. So do not make any rapid motions, and keep your hands in plain sight.

Try your best to calmly answer any questions that the police ask. Be polite, allow the officer to speak, and address him or her as "officer." Try not to show nervousness or frustration, and, most important, do not be rude or abrasive.

Tell the police officer your name and address. Remember that officers may not be experienced, are only trying to do their job, and may be tense because they themselves are afraid.

If the police stop you, remember that you have the right to remain silent. You do not need to speak if officers ask questions that you do not want to answer about what you are doing or anything that could make them suspect you of a crime. However, to prove to the officers that you are not trying to resist them or their questioning, simply say, "I have a right to remain silent." Then you should remain silent until you have a chance to talk to your parents or to a lawyer. Use your best judgment—if the situation seems easy to resolve, it would be wise to talk to the police about what happened and clear up any misunderstanding. Giving them the information that they ask for may end the encounter quickly and squelch their suspicions about you. But if there is any chance that you are under suspicion of a serious crime or violation, you might want to remain silent for your own protection, even if the police try to pressure you into talking. Anything you say can be used in court.

If you are stopped by the police and believe that your rights have been violated, try to remember the names of the officers, their badge numbers, the license plate number of the patrol car, and the place and time of the incident so that, if necessary, you can make a complaint. Many police departments have civilian complaint review procedures under which you can take confidential action against an officer who you believe has abused your rights. If you think your rights have been violated, you may want to file this type of confidential complaint so that the police department can hold officers accountable and prevent them from engaging in abusive behavior in the future. If the department is not responsive to your complaint, you can contact a community group that may be able to complain on your behalf or enable you to find other ways to make your story heard.

THE ISSUE OF POLICE BRUTALITY

Abusive searches are not reasonable searches. However, in many well-publicized cases, police officers have gone so far as to shoot unarmed civilians and then claim that they were afraid for their lives and thus had reasonable grounds to use deadly force. Police are allowed to use whatever force is necessary

Demonstrators protest some incidents of alleged police brutality in Los Angeles, California. Police officers can use deadly force if they believe a person in question poses an immediate danger to them or the people around them.

to restrain a person for an arrest, so resisting police with force can escalate an encounter. Resisting the police, even verbally, is dangerous. Even though you may be anxious or afraid, keeping calm is extremely important if you ever have an encounter with the police. Officers may be new on the job. They may be as afraid of you as you are of them. Do not give them any reason to overreact and resort to violence. Move very slowly, and talk clearly so that there are no misunderstandings, even if it is to say that you have the right to remain silent.

Young people are the victims of police brutality more often than those in any other age group. Why do you think this is the case? One reason why is that teens may be more likely to take part in dangerous or irresponsible activities. Another reason may be fear on the part of the officers in dealing with such situations. As a teen, remember that you have rights within the limits of the law. Following the law should ensure that your personal rights are preserved.

PRIVACY AND JUVENILE CURFEWS

One of the most obvious issues surrounding teen privacy is the juvenile curfew. Towns across America are allowed to designate a time during which people under the age of eighteen are not allowed outside. Quite often, these curfews are enacted at sundown, or at 9:00 or 10:00 PM so that young people are discouraged from hanging out and causing problems. Even if young people are allowed out by their parents, they are breaking the law if they are not following local curfew laws. Consequences for not following the laws might be arrest, overnight detention, suspension of driving privileges, or community service. Their parents might face a criminal fine or community service, or they might have to take parenting classes.

Juvenile curfew laws pose one of the most serious threats to the constitutional rights of young adults. Although curfew laws have been around for a hundred years, they have mostly been used only in temporary emergencies. Today, juvenile curfews are becoming increasingly popular, especially in communities that are concerned about gang violence. These curfew laws usually say that individuals under the age of sixteen cannot be outside of their homes after a certain hour at night, usually eleven o'clock. If they are caught, they face overnight detention, suspension of driving privileges, community service hours, or even arrest.

Cities or counties pass curfew laws out of fear of juvenile crime, to protect juveniles from crime, and to support parents' authority over their children. These are understandable concerns, and these laws keep getting passed. On the other hand, no studies have shown any sure connection between these laws and an actual reduction in juvenile crime. The fact is, the people fined or arrested under curfew laws are not guilty of any crime, only of being outside. Some of the laws do not even create an exception when children have permission from their parents to stay outside, though most say that being outside with an adult is allowed. Not only do the laws infringe upon the rights of minors, but they also may limit the parents' right to raise their children as they see fit.

There is also a serious concern that police will enforce these curfew laws in a discriminatory way, arresting only minority children or poor children after hours. Some of these laws give police a great deal of discretion in deciding whether to fine minors, accept an excuse, take them to a special juvenile curfew center, or arrest them. Police are already accused of arresting far more minority children than nonminority children, and judges are accused of giving minority children harsher sentences than nonminorities who commit the same offenses. Some curfew laws are criticized because they may give police more opportunity to act in a biased way.

A good example of how the courts treat curfew laws was demonstrated by a 1999 federal lawsuit, *Hutchins v. District of Columbia*, which involved a curfew law in the District of Columbia. The law prohibited those under the age of seventeen from being in public areas unaccompanied by an assigned adult of at least twenty-one years of age from 11:00 PM to 6:00 AM Sunday through Thursday, and from 12:01 am to 6:00 AM on Friday and Saturday. Nine children and four parents sued the District of Columbia, arguing that the law restricted the rights of free movement, free speech, freedom of assembly, and the right to be free from unreasonable searches and seizures. The court considered both the rights of minors and the interest of the District in protecting minors from harm. The court upheld the law, saying that the District has broad authority over children, and that this law was not too vague.

The Supreme Court has repeatedly decided not to review lower court decisions upholding similar juvenile curfew laws. However, the Court did step in, in 1999, to end an anti-loitering law that it felt gave police too much power over citizens in Chicago, Illinois. The city had put a law into place in 1992 that was intended to help deal with the problems of gangs, drugs, and prostitution. Police were allowed to tell anyone they felt was loitering on the streets to move on, and if the people did not move on to the police's satisfaction, they were allowed to issue warrants for dispersal and even for arrest. In just a few years, they issued more than eighty-nine thousand orders to disperse and made forty-two thousand arrests. Most of the arrests were of young minorities. A lawsuit regarding the anti-loitering law reached the Supreme Court, and the Court decided that it was unconstitutional to give police so much power over the public. The crime and gang problems in Chicago are still very serious to this day, however. Although the right to privacy must be maintained for Americans, the safety of citizens must be equally considered. The courts consider each and every case that comes before them to determine the fairest balance possible.

RACIAL PROFILING AND PRIVACY

Police are not allowed to search people simply because they are minorities, or because they are young

Sheriff deputies in Arizona spot-check people after the state's new immigration law went into effect. A U.S. district judge ruled in July 2010 that major portions of the law encroached upon federal immigration enforcement.

and male. These are not reasonable grounds to suspect criminal activity. Yet more and more studies have shown that police departments choose to stop or arrest people based on their race. The practice of suspecting a person of criminal activity based only on his or her skin color or race is called racial profiling. It has happened for years to African-American and Hispanic males, who have been accused of crimes such as weapon or drug possession, theft, and violent crimes. However, since September 11, 2001, more citizens of Middle Eastern descent have become victims of racial profiling as well. It is true that on 9/11, nineteen Middle Eastern males carried out the biggest terrorist attack on American soil. But should the rights of millions of innocent Middle Eastern Americans be taken away in the search for terrorists? The laws for all Americans changed after 9/11, when the USA PATRIOT Act was signed into law on October 26, 2001. Racial profiling is just one of the results of increased security meant to protect Americans from harm. How far should the law go to protect Americans if it must invade the privacy rights of all Americans in the process? This is not an easy question to answer. Racial profiling makes the issue even more complex. Some people who are stopped at airports as a result of racial profiling are not even American citizens. Does that make it OK to stop them for suspicion of crimes based on their race or religion?

The racial profiling of Middle Easterners was not the first time that the rights of American citizens were violated as a result of political involvement. During World War II (1939–1945), Japanese Americans along the Pacific coast of the United States were relocated to internment camps after Japan attacked Pearl Harbor, Hawaii, on December 7, 1941. The internment of Japanese Americans was uneven throughout the country; it focused most on the geographic location closest to Pearl Harbor. It was not until 1988 that the U.S.

government apologized for this action against the civil rights and privacy of its fellow Americans.

Today, many religious and civil rights groups across the country are involved in trying to put an end to the practice of racial profiling. Contacting a local office of the American Civil Liberties Union (ACLU) can help citizens deal with any racial profiling that they may witness in their everyday lives.

Other Kinds of Searches

Police searches include more than just officers looking into your pockets or your bag. Recording your voice, watching over your property, or taking samples of your blood are also considered searches. The Supreme Court has said that taking a sample of your handwriting is not a search, however, because whenever you write, you give your handwriting to the public. Similarly, people leave fingerprints wherever they go, so when police take a fingerprint, it is not considered a search.

But anything that violates your bodily integrity is a search and must be conducted reasonably. Stomach pumping, strip searches and seizures searches, and body cavity checks are generally unconstitutional when there are not strong reasons to perform them. Blood tests and urinalysis for drugs can also be considered searches. Breath testing is also a search. Any search that physically invades one's space requires probable cause or a reasonable suspicion.

A person's property is private, but if the public can view part of that property, the police can use information without probable cause. For example, a farmer in Kentucky had a fenced-off field, but police could observe marijuana growing in the field from the surrounding property. The Supreme Court held that "an individual may not legitimately demand privacy for activities conducted out of doors in fields...except in the area immediately surrounding the home."

The Supreme Court has also analyzed the issue of people being able to search through someone's garbage. The Court has said that garbage is not protected by the Fourth Amendment because, although it contains personal information, people have thrown it away and thus given it to the public.

The Beginnings of Government Surveillance

Surveillance is one of the most troubling kinds of search because you never know when someone might be watching you. Supreme Court Justice William H. Brennan once wrote, "Electronic surveillance strikes deeper than at the ancient feeling that a man's home is his castle; it strikes at the freedom of communication, a postulate of our free society."

The first time that the American public became concerned about the government surveying and interfering with their private matters was during the Cold War. Starting in the 1950s, relations between the United States and the Soviet Union were bitter and hostile. James Bond–type tactics were originally designed for use in foreign intelligence, to spy on enemies in the Soviet Union during the Cold War. But shortly thereafter, the U.S. government decided to use these same tactics in America, against communists and other political and social groups. For more than thirty years, without any authorization, the U.S. government engaged in surveillance of the everyday activities of some of its citizens. This illegal surveillance was often carried out by the Federal Bureau of Investigation (FBI) in the name of national security, but the practice began to go too far and caused abuses of civil liberties and privacy.

Early in the 1950s, the FBI, led by J. Edgar Hoover, developed a secret program to fight the Communist Party in America, which was a legal political party. The FBI spied on members of the party, disrupting their daily lives in the process. The FBI used Central Intelligence Agency (CIA) spy programs in the Soviet Union as its model. The FBI's infiltration program was later called COINTELPRO, which stood for counterintelligence program. It was designed to function as a kind of domestic counterintelligence, which would "expose, disrupt, and otherwise neutralize" political groups the FBI felt were a threat to America. Wiretaps

were placed in the homes of members of the
Communist Party, and private conversations were
taped. People were fired or arrested based on conversations that were taped without their knowledge.
They were taped not because they were suspected of
being a criminal, but because they were part of a
political party that the government was at odds with.
Not only were members of the Communist Party targeted, but later during the 1960s, members of the civil
rights movement also were targeted.

These eavesdropping methods were abuses to citizens' right to privacy, and there were no laws against
them at the time. It was not until 1961 that the
Supreme Court created some constitutional protections against government surveillance. In the case of
Silverman v. United States, it decided that federal agents
could not arrest someone based on conversations
recorded in that person's home without permission. In
1966, in *Osborne v. United States*, it held that some
eavesdropping is permissible, but that police must
receive permission from a judge before they eavesdrop.
Finally, in *Katz v. United States*, in 1967, the Supreme
Court held that the Fourth Amendment, which protects
against unreasonable searches and seizures, also protects against eavesdropping. Eavesdropping is a kind
of seizure—a seizure of one's words.

In 1968, Congress passed the Omnibus Crime
Control and Safe Streets Act in order to give meaning

to the Supreme Court's decisions by making clear what kinds of eavesdropping would be permitted. President Lyndon B. Johnson introduced the bill with a ringing endorsement of privacy rights:

> We should protect what Justice Brandeis called the "right most valued by civilized men,"—the right of privacy. We should outlaw all wiretapping—public and private—whenever and wherever it occurs, *except when the security of the nation is at stake*—and only then with the strictest safeguards. We should exercise the full reach of our Constitutional powers to outlaw electronic "bugging" and "snooping".

However, the law that was passed—which is still the law today—has some very large loopholes. Wiretapping and other forms of eavesdropping can be performed when any federal felony is involved, and consequently, there is a long list of crimes where eavesdropping is permissible. The attorney general can approve wiretaps or eavesdropping. Eavesdropping is also allowed when "national security is at stake."

Even to this day, the question of what constitutes national security is difficult to answer. President Richard M. Nixon claimed that he should be permitted to eavesdrop on people whom he felt were a threat to him. Nixon claimed that the president could

SECTION 215 OF THE USA PATRIOT ACT, CALLED THE "LIBRARY PROVISION"

The Uniting and Strengthening America by Providing Appropriate Tools Required to Intercept and Obstruct Terrorism Act, better known as the USA PATRIOT Act, was introduced into Congress less than one week after the September 11, 2001, terrorist attacks in the United States. President George W. Bush signed the act into law on October 26, 2001. The PATRIOT Act expanded law enforcement's powers in surveillance and investigation, including regulations concerning electronic communications, computer fraud and abuse, foreign intelligence surveillance, and family education rights. It also contained Section 215. This provision allows law enforcement agents to solicit "tangible things," a wide range of private business records without warrants, including a person's library records. The

U.S. Attorney General Eric Holder spoke out against a lawsuit in California about warrantless wiretapping. He believes that the lawsuit threatens to expose ongoing intelligence work by law enforcement and it must be thrown out.

American Civil Liberties Union, among other groups, called for the act's Section 215 to be restricted to suspected terrorists only. In February 2010, President Barack Obama reauthorized several provisions of the PATRIOT Act for a one-year extension, including Section 215, without adding any new checks and balances to the act. Consequently, what if you wanted to read about September 11 and the terrorists, look at a tourist's guide to Malaysia or Afghanistan, flip through a flight-training instruction book on how to fly a commercial airplane, or check out a copy of the Qur'an (the holy book of Islam)? What would your library record tell law enforcement authorities about you?

eavesdrop whenever some national interest was at stake. In 1972, the Supreme Court in *United States v. U.S. District Court, Eastern District of Michigan* held that even the president cannot wiretap without a warrant and that the national security exception is reserved only for the most dire situations.

The Watergate Scandal, the series of events that led to President Nixon's resignation, began in June 1972. That's when Nixon's staffers were caught trying to install electronic bugs and wiretaps at the Democratic Party's presidential campaign headquarters, which were located in the Watergate office complex in Washington, D.C. In the investigation that followed, the public learned that Nixon had performed illegal

wiretaps of journalists and high government officials who were critical of him. He even had his own workers ransack the offices of a psychiatrist in Los Angeles, California, to try to obtain the private records of a critic of his administration.

Government Surveillance Today

The world has changed a lot since the years of the Nixon administration. There are still issues of government surveillance and questions about the right to privacy. However, they now concern the rights of every individual, regardless of the person's political affiliation or beliefs. Despite the protections that the Constitution provides, the USA PATRIOT Act of 2001 lessened some of the privacy rights that were once guaranteed. More government searches of telephones, e-mails, financial records, and medical records are permitted than ever before. Many of the provisions of the act were meant to lapse about four years after they were put into place. But months before the act was set to expire, many of the provisions were made permanent or were reauthorized.

Government authorities have a right to monitor some correspondence on the Internet or via cell phones and landline phones. Many of these officials reason that these methods should be able to be used

After a car bomb attempt in New York City's Times Square, the police department increased surveillance efforts by using security cameras in the streets of New York.

because they protect ordinary citizens. They argue that any small loss of privacy is far outweighed by the protection that citizens receive.

More than two thousand criminal wiretaps were authorized in 2009. Most were done through mobile phones in an effort to catch people suspected of drug dealing. But how are average, law-abiding citizens at risk of losing their right to privacy? In 2009, a federal court ruled that telecommunications companies must cooperate with government agencies seeking to intercept phone calls overseas and e-mails of Americans who are suspected of terrorist activities or of taking part in spy activities. Only a suspicion is needed, and no evidence of wrongdoing must be proved ahead of time. This puts the power into the hands of the government at the expense of the citizens, similar to the FBI activities conducted in the 1950s regarding the Communist Party.

Local police are also allowed to confiscate a person's computer if the person is suspected of a crime. The computer records can be sorted through to give law officials either the evidence they need to link the person to criminal behavior or clear that person of suspicion.

In 2010, California courts allowed law enforcement officials to place global positioning system (GPS) devices on the vehicles of people suspected of criminal activity. These devices may be placed without a warrant and can be used to track the activity of the people under suspicion. This method led to the arrest of a man who was suspected of growing marijuana. The GPS device repeatedly tracked his car's movement to a remote rural location where marijuana was being grown. The man was unknowingly being tracked, and the GPS evidence was enough to allow officers to arrest him.

In September 2010, the *New York Times* reported that the Obama administration planned to submit to Congress in 2011 a bill that would give the federal government and law enforcement agencies broad new regulations for the Internet. The bill requires all services that enable communications, such as encrypted e-mail transmitters (BlackBerry, etc.), social networking sites (Facebook, etc.), and software that enables direct peer-to-peer messaging (Skype, etc.), to be capable of complying if they are served with a wiretap order. The rule would include being able to intercept and unscramble encrypted messages. Federal authorities say that with the public's increased use of online communications, law enforcement officials are finding it more difficult to wiretap criminals and terrorists. They also believe that when the bill becomes law, it will "prevent the erosion of their investigative powers." Problems concerning how to balance the nation's security with citizens' right to privacy continue. The line between protection and rights violations seems to be thinning. It is the job of Americans to make sure that their rights are not violated.

CHAPTER 4

I n general, teenagers have much weaker privacy protections than adults. School officials can often search a young person's belongings with less than the reasonable suspicion that police officers must have. Schools can sometimes disclose information against a teen's will. And in some states, parental consent is needed if a teenage girl tries to obtain an abortion. The sad truth is that being young usually means having fewer rights, but knowing about privacy rights means that a person can protect himself or herself. There are things that young people can do to challenge violations of their privacy, or at least raise people's awareness of the issue.

SCHOOL AUTHORITIES

Schools have rules for good reasons. They seek to maintain order among the students, as well as ensuring that students abide by the law. Many schools have rules that prevent students from carrying any kind of drug on them for any reason. Any doctor-prescribed medications must be provided by the parents and administered by a school nurse. However, the enforcement of these rules can sometimes go too far. In one Arizona middle school, a thirteen-year-old girl named Savana Redding was strip-searched by school authorities who were looking for a prescription tab of ibuprofen that another student claimed was provided by Redding. In 2009, in *Safford Unified School District v. Redding*, the Supreme Court decided that this search went too far and violated the girl's right to privacy, as guaranteed in the Fourth Amendment.

Like the police, school authorities may conduct searches that infringe on your right to privacy. As you know, schools have increasingly invaded students' privacy by searching their belongings, conducting drug tests, and installing metal detectors. Schools are often allowed to ban weapons, electronic pagers, and cell phones. They are trying to cope with drugs and violence, especially in the wake of the rising number of school shootings. They want to be sure that their students are safe. But as a result, schools may overreact and end up creating an environment that is hostile to learning.

It is legal for schools to use metal detectors. Perhaps one reason why metal detectors are so widely accepted in schools is that they are so common in many other public places, such as airports and courthouses. More and more schools are installing walk-through metal detectors or are using handheld metal detectors to check individual students. They are

Honor student Savana Redding leaves the U.S. Supreme Court Building after her case was heard in 2009. Redding was strip-searched by middle school officials who were looking for prescription-strength ibuprofen pills.

installing video surveillance cameras in public parts of the school. Some schools are even asking the police to go undercover, pretending to be students in an effort to catch drug dealers. Plainclothes officers may also patrol a school.

The right to privacy for students goes back a generation or more. In the 1969 case *Tinker v. Des Moines Independent Community School District*, the Supreme Court said, "It can hardly be argued that either students or teachers shed their constitutional rights…at the schoolhouse gate." However, students have fewer rights in school than they do on the street. The first time that the Supreme Court ruled on privacy in schools, it conducted a "balancing test" to decide whether a school's interest in finding out if students are doing illegal things was on balance more important than the interests of the students in having privacy. The Court ruled that on balance, a school's interests are more important. Over and over again, when courts balance the rights of students against a school's interest in safety, the court ends up on the school's side.

The 1985 Supreme Court case *New Jersey v. T. L. O.* involved a fourteen-year-old freshman in high school who was found sitting on the sinks in the school bathroom smoking cigarettes with a friend. In those days, smoking was allowed at this high school, but only in certain areas and not in the bathrooms. The friend admitted that she was smoking and was given a three-day suspension. T. L. O., whose name was kept private by the courts, was taken to the principal's office and denied smoking anything at all. The principal asked to see her purse, which he had done many times before. He searched her purse and found cigarettes. Then he dug deeper and found cigarette rolling papers, marijuana, a pipe, and assorted drug paraphernalia, including a list of names and letters concerning marijuana sales. T. L. O. was suspended for ten days, and the police entered the case.

The government brought charges against her in juvenile court for delinquency because of possession of marijuana with intent to distribute. T. L. O.'s parents hired a lawyer, and the student argued that the evidence the principal found in her purse should not be used against her in court because it had been obtained illegally. She said that the principal's search violated her Fourth Amendment rights against an unreasonable search or seizure because he had not obtained a warrant signed by a judge.

The case passed through three New Jersey courts, and each decided the case a different way. It finally went to the Supreme Court because the Court had never before decided if the Fourth Amendment even applied to searches by school officials.

Interestingly, T. L. O. was not excited about the Supreme Court hearing her case. By this time, she had graduated and did not want to be remembered for the rest of her life as the girl who was caught smoking in the bathroom. T. L. O., ironically, wanted her story kept private. Would you want something that happened to you to become an important legal case? Would you want to be known for helping to defend the rights of other students, or would you rather get on with your life and not have your story be in the public eye?

In 1985, the Supreme Court decided that students have "legitimate expectations of privacy" and the Fourth Amendment does apply. But the Court also ruled that the search of T. L. O. was constitutional. It said that only "reasonable" ground is necessary for a school search, which is less than the full "probable cause" required for searches under the Fourth Amendment. While in some respects students have less protection in schools, school authorities are supposed to maintain a proper learning environment where students do not live in fear of being searched for no reason. On one hand, the Supreme Court said that school officials are different from police and that requiring probable cause would "unduly interfere with the maintenance of the swift and informal disciplinary procedures needed in schools." The Court held that school authorities do not always need to obtain a warrant in order to conduct a reasonable search. It also said that schools must consider first if the search is justified, and second, if the way it is conducted is reasonable, given the circumstances. On the other hand, the Court said that schools must make some effort to limit their searches so that they do only what is needed in order to find what they are looking for. The Supreme Court said:

[A] search will be permissible in its scope when the measures adopted are reasonably related to the objectives of the search and not excessively intrusive in light of the age and sex of the student and the nature of the infraction.

Some state courts have been more stringent than the Supreme Court; for example, Louisiana requires a full probable cause for searching students. Most state courts follow the Supreme Court, though, and require only a reasonable suspicion. Although school authorities are supposed to have a reason for a search and to make sure that searches are not too intrusive, many very intrusive searches have been allowed by courts. Courts are often deferential to school authorities, which means that school authorities do not need to have a very specific or strong reason to search a student. But school officials do have to have some reason to search a student and must suspect that particular student of breaking a law or school rule. They cannot generally suspect that some students are up to no good. They must be able to explain why they thought a student was doing something wrong. To make their case for reasonable suspicion, school officials can rely on things like a student's school record, information from other students, the seriousness of the problem faced by the school, or prior encounters between a student and school officials.

Some searches, such as mass searches and strip searches, are inherently very intrusive and might be more limited under *T. L. O.'s* rule against "excessively intrusive" searches. One school in New York strip-searched an entire fifth grade class because three dollars were missing. In 1977, a federal court, in *Bellnier v. Lund*, found the search unreasonable. Some courts say that there has to be much more suspicion for school authorities to perform a more intrusive search.

Searches of lockers and desks are allowed. Since these searches are less intrusive than frisking a student, courts tend to permit locker and desk searches more often. Some state courts are more protective of students' privacy and say that the same suspicion is needed to search a locker as to search a student. A few states even have laws that protect students from random locker searches. Find out if your school district has a policy on locker or desk searches.

SEARCHES PERMITTED IN SCHOOLS

The line between what is allowed and what is not allowed by school officials can be extremely blurry. Here are some examples of what is permitted in terms of student searches by school officials:

- A school official who smells marijuana or cigarette smoke has the right to search an area to find the source of the odor and the substances in question. This includes searches of lockers or students' personal belongings. The odor counts as reasonable suspicion for the search.

Many U.S. schools use metal detectors to help ensure school safety. Although metal detectors do not totally eliminate violence in schools, they can help detect small guns and knives.

- Some state courts have decided that lockers are school property, and therefore, they may be searched for any reason or for no reason at all. School officials have been known to search lockers for weapons, drugs, and other illegal goods. Students do not often have a right to claim protection under the Fourth Amendment in these cases because the locker is the school's property and the possession of the goods is prohibited on school property.

- A search of a student's personal property is permitted if school authorities have a reason to suspect illegal activity, illegal possession of goods, or a disregard for school rules. The search might include going through a student's backpack, pockets, or coat. The nature of the search should not unnecessarily violate the individual's personal space. Strip searches are often not permitted unless the circumstances are extreme and the case particularly endangers the safety of the school.

- Metal detectors are permitted to be used in school searches, particularly for guns or knives. Students should not be singled out for these searches without a good reason, but random searches are usually allowed to be applied to the entire population of the school. Courts usually permit these random searches because the interest of school safety usually outweighs the interest of an individual's privacy.

- When a student is found in an area of the school where he or she should not be, such as outside during class or in the bathroom without a hall pass, school officials usually have the right to search the student, including searches of his or her wallet, purse, or backpack.

SEARCHES NOT PERMITTED IN SCHOOLS

Although the above examples of searches are normally allowed in schools, there are cases where courts have decided that schools have gone too far and violated students' rights. The following are specific cases in which courts sided with the students who felt their rights were being violated:

- A school principal searched a student who was repeatedly late to school and carrying a bag with an "odd-looking bulge." The principal asked to see what was in the bag, but the student refused to open it and said that the principal needed a warrant. In this case, *In re William G* (1985), the

California Supreme Court said that there was no reasonable suspicion. (But this case seems almost exactly like the situation in *New Jersey v. T. L. O.,* where the Supreme Court said that the search was allowed.)

- Twice in one hour, a student was observed going into a restroom. Seconds later, another student would leave the restroom. A school official then conducted a drug search. The New York Court of Appeals ruled that this was an innocent activity and that conducting unnecessary searches causes students too much psychological damage.

- A school made all students participating in a band trip agree that their luggage could be searched without any reason. A Washington State court, in *Kuehn v. Renton School District* (1985), said that this kind of mass search without any reasonable suspicion is not allowed.

In some cases, there is little difference between some of the searches that courts allow and others that they don't allow. The law is much divided in this area, and it may depend on your state courts' understanding of what is appropriate for officials to do in schools. So remember, school officials must have a "reasonable basis" for their searches, but usually just having some suspicions about a particular person is enough.

What happens if a search is illegal? Sometimes, a court will not accept the evidence that police or school officials found during the search. This rule is called the exclusionary rule because evidence that is obtained illegally is "excluded" from being introduced in court. However, the exclusionary rule probably will not apply for the purposes of a school disciplinary hearing, so school authorities can still punish you even if their search was illegal. Your school may have a policy that defines how it treats illegal searches for the purposes of evidence used in disciplinary hearings. So you can check to be sure how your school deals with this issue.

WHAT STUDENTS SHOULD KNOW IF THEY OR THEIR BELONGINGS ARE BEING SEARCHED

Because it is clear that students in a school environment are subject to more personal searches than adults are, they should know that they still have a right to protect themselves against personal violations. Here are some things that students should know about their rights, even if they are subject to personal searches:

- Students should understand the seriousness of bringing drugs or weapons to school. These crimes can be met with harsh consequences, including probation and jail time, both of which can affect a person's legal record for the rest of his or her life.

- Resisting a search by a school official can cause the official to call in the police. Instead of risking this involvement, simply allow the search so that you can clear your name in the incident.

- Students do have a right to remain silent during a search. Students who express that they do not consent to a search or they have a right to remain silent can possibly avoid having information used against them in court. In the event that a court finds the search unlawful, you will not have given up your rights by verbally allowing the search first or by voluntarily providing information.

SCHOOLS AND LAW ENFORCEMENT

The situations discussed above involve school officials, not the police or other law enforcement agencies. Of course, police officers are already inside some schools, working undercover. Schools can allow the police to question students in school. Often, the school will allow police officers to call students out of class to discuss something with them. As with school authorities, students have the right to remain silent when talking to law enforcement. In some situations, they may choose to remain silent until they speak with their parents or a lawyer. In many other cases, however, a student's cooperation with the police can be helpful in keeping schools safe. Students who have reported to police that classmates have written "hit lists" of students whom they intend to hurt or kill have actually helped police catch students ahead of time before they were able to harm anyone. If you are being accused of a crime, however, do not lie. Get the help of a parent or lawyer, if necessary. Try not to be intimidated if the officers say that they will not let you leave if you do not talk to them or that not speaking will harm you. Remember that the intention of the police is to keep your school safe.

Some cities and states have laws limiting the schools' ability to let police question students, sometimes saying that a school official must be with the student who is questioned to be certain that the student is not threatened. Some school districts require calling in the police when there is a crime on school grounds, especially in cases of drug or weapon possession. Find out what your school's rules are regarding police involvement.

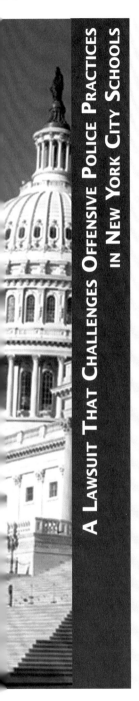

A LAWSUIT THAT CHALLENGES OFFENSIVE POLICE PRACTICES IN NEW YORK CITY SCHOOLS

In January 2010, the ACLU and the New York Civil Liberties Union (NYCLU) filed a class-action federal lawsuit challenging the alleged practices and conduct of police officers and school safety officers serving in the New York Police Department's School Safety Division. The suit, representing five middle school and high school students who reportedly were physically abused and wrongfully arrested, challenges the School Safety Division's policies and practices of "unlawful seizing and arresting schoolchildren, in violation of the Fourth Amendment and state law." The safety personnel allegedly arrested students for minor infractions of school rules that were not criminal actions, handcuffed and locked them in secluded rooms without parental or teacher consent and without probable cause, and removed the children who misbehaved in school without teacher or parental consent, taking them to hospitals for emergency psychiatric evaluations. According to the ACLU, the lawsuit, *B. H. et al v. City of New York*, seeks to return disciplinary decisions back to New York City's school administrators; have mandatory training of safety personnel, especially conduct relating to arrests, searches, and use of force (preparation would include learning the difference between the disciplinary code and the penal code); create a transparent and meaningful method for students and parents to file complaints against members of the School Safety Division; and rewrite the policies and steps regarding discipline of safety personnel who have been found to have committed an abuse.

Schools and Drug Testing

More and more schools are using drug tests to combat drug use. A drug or alcohol test is a kind of search. Like other searches, drug tests must be done for a reason; random or unreasonable drug tests may be unconstitutional.

The Supreme Court, in the 1995 case *Vernonia v. Acton*, said that student athletes can be tested for drugs at random and without any suspicion because athletic programs are voluntary. Athletes are said to give up their privacy expectations because they volunteered to participate in the sport. Justice Antonin Scalia, who wrote the opinion, also said that athletes have less of an expectation of privacy because they change clothes and shower together. The Court said that since athletes can be role models, it is especially important to be sure that they do not use drugs. The reasoning in *Vernonia* has been extended to include all other extracurricular activities.

However, since this landmark case, students and coaches alike have admitted that random drug testing does not seem to help prevent student athletes from using drugs. Regardless of the effects of the law, it is doubtful that it will be changed. Student athletes are unlikely to be given their rights back and allowed to volunteer in drug tests, rather than be forced to take them. One of the problems with giving up rights is that they are rarely given back. Courts will often accept schools' arguments that invading students' privacy is necessary to ensure a safe learning environment.

PERSONAL INFORMATION AND PRIVACY

Aside from searches, schools are increasingly talking about releasing confidential information about students who they decide are "troubled." After the shootings in 1999 at Columbine High School in Colorado and at other schools, many teachers have decided that for their own protection, and for the protection of all their students, they need to know in advance who the troubled kids are. They want guidance counselors to warn them if a student is having severe emotional problems that might be an indication of anger and violent tendencies. Teachers say that this will give them advance warning about possible problems and encourage more people on the faculty to get involved at an earlier stage in helping these students. On the other hand, it could mean that teachers will become unnecessarily afraid of students or develop unfairly negative impressions of students. Releasing this information may also discourage students from ever visiting guidance counselors in the first place, since most students don't want all of their teachers to know the details of their private problems. Breaching this trust between a student and guidance counselor may ultimately do more harm than good. Students may be less likely to receive needed help.

Some school districts try to draw a line between the teachers' desire to know if they are in any danger and the students' privacy. Teachers are told if a student has made violent threats, what treatment the student is receiving, and how long the student will be suspended. But no other personal or psychological information is given. Again, privacy rights are balanced with public interests. Is this the right kind of balance? Should other students also have a right to know if one of their classmates might have violent tendencies? Or that more protections for students' rights could be created? What role should the troubled student's family play in deciding what information is released?

After the Columbine shooting, people wondered: Why hadn't the school noticed that one of its students had a Web site featuring racist symbols, hate speech, and threats? Should schools be monitoring the Internet and watching over the speech of students? Should they monitor use of the Internet on school computers? What about the free speech rights of the students? In one such incident, a school suspended a third-grade student for submitting a fortune cookie for a project with the words "You will die an honor-able death" on it. The student was just a martial arts

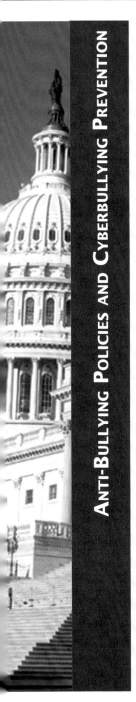

ANTI-BULLYING POLICIES AND CYBERBULLYING PREVENTION

After the suicides of several teenagers who were bullied at school or were the victims of cyberbullying and invasion of privacy, including Megan Meier in 2006 and Phoebe Prince and Tyler Clementi in 2010, various schools and colleges have passed antibullying policies to protect students from being harassed at school or in dormitory rooms. There are about forty-five state legislatures that have passed laws that make bullying or cyberbullying a crime.

The U.S. Congress introduced legislation in 2009 to address concerns about recent cyber-bullying attacks to help protect young people at school and on the Internet. Named the Megan Meier Cyberbullying Prevention Act, for the thirteen-year-old who committed suicide after being bullied and coerced on the Internet, the bill, according to OpenCongress.org, is still making its way through the legislative process. When and if it is enacted, the bill would amend the "federal criminal code to impose criminal penalties on anyone who transmits in interstate or foreign commerce a communication intended to coerce, intimidate, harass, or cause substantial emotional distress to another person, using electronic means to support severe, repeated, and hostile behavior." The crime would be punishable by a fine and up to two years in prison. Opponents of the bill, however, say it impacts on the freedom of speech as protected by the First Amendment. Currently, there is no federal law that explicitly makes bullying a crime. There are antistalking, criminal harassment, and civil rights laws, though, that can be used to address bullying violations.

fan, but the school decided that the message was threatening and the student should be punished. Should just mentioning death in school be an offense?

The high school yearbook is a private source of information that police can use to combat crime. Police use student photos from high school yearbooks in police lineups. They show the yearbooks to victims and witnesses of crimes for identification of the alleged perpetrator. Recently, the ACLU and other groups complained when the New York Police Department collected yearbooks from all of the city's high schools. Do you think this is an improper use of people's images? Students never consented to have their photos released, but police say that when juveniles are suspected in crimes, yearbooks are a comprehensive source that schools can supply of images of young people in the area.

The Privacy of Student Records

Students have a right to access any records in their student files at a public school. They also have a right to stop a school from releasing their records without their consent. This is important because, otherwise, a teacher or school administrator could threaten a student with changing his or her record or writing a harmful college or job recommendation. Some states or school districts have rules against teachers using recommendations to punish students for their political beliefs. Teachers have written letters complaining that a student is politically active, antireligious, or does not respect the flag. These kinds of personal comments are inappropriate not just because they are harmful; they also discourage students from exercising the right of free speech.

In 1974, Congress passed the Family Educational Rights Privacy Act (FERPA), also called the Buckley Amendment. Before this federal law was passed, students could never see their records, much less find out if there was anything improper in them or stop the school from disclosing them. Now, students over eighteen years old have a right to "inspect and review" their records, and parents can obtain the students' records with their permission. A school must respond to a person's request to view records within a reasonable time—not more than forty-five days, and often much less, under some states' laws. Some records, like psychiatric records, can be seen only by parents and not by students. Students may see letters of recommendation, but not if they have waived the right to see them— many colleges ask that students waive that right.

Students also have a right to ask that incorrect information in their records be corrected. They can meet with school officials to have the information corrected, and if schools refuse, they can request a formal hearing about it. If a school is improperly disclosing student records or denies a student access to his or her records, that student can make a complaint to the U.S. Department of Education. The Buckley Amendment also makes it harder for schools to give out information without the student's permission. A school can release information only with the student's written consent, unless it is just showing the record to another teacher. A parent can review a record before it is sent to a school to which a student is transferring. The Buckley Amendment does not apply to private schools, though. State laws may regulate private schools, however.

WORKING TOWARD A CHANGE AT SCHOOL

Even if school authorities think that they have a reasonable policy, you may still feel that your privacy is being infringed on in a serious way—and you may be right. Although what the school is doing may be legally permitted, the student may think that what the school is doing is wrong. If students and parents express their concern over invasion of privacy, the school may change its policy. Bear in mind that it is difficult at times to challenge even an illegal practice at a school. While students have rights, having those rights enforced may be difficult. The principal or other school officials may even try to retaliate against a student if he or she threatens litigation. Of course, legal services groups or groups like the ACLU may be able to stand up for student rights. Standing up for legal rights also benefits the lives of all students whose rights are injured in schools. Many people, including students, have made sacrifices in many ways in order to defend constitutional rights. But be sure to think carefully about your options before challenging school actions, and talk about your decision with your parents and maybe with a lawyer. Here are some other things that students can do:

- Start an ongoing dialogue about a privacy issue. Discuss with other students the school's treatment of privacy issues and find out if people have been searched or have had their privacy rights violated in some way. See if others are concerned and want to help. Maybe the student government can get involved in organizing students or circulating petitions and information about students' rights.

- Create a new student group or get together a group of students concerned about the rights of students.

- Decide on an agenda. Are drug tests the problem, or locker searches, or use of undercover police officers? Is the school reluctant to admit what its policies are in regard to student privacy? Is there a particular school official who acts abusively toward students? Schools are supposed to create a safe learning environment. Students have the right to demand fair and respectful treatment from school authorities.

- Have students sign a petition protesting a school policy or practice that may infringe on students' right to privacy. Set up a table with information about students' rights. Write letters or postcards to state officials or school board officials, explaining the students' concerns.

- Talk to teachers or guidance counselors who may be concerned or helpful. Maybe they can give advice about approaching the administration with a problem. If there are teachers sympathetic to the students' cause, a faculty adviser could sponsor the students' work and share information about school policies and procedures. Also talk to parents: Parents are very influential because they can bring up issues at PTA meetings or other meetings with school authorities. They should be very concerned about how students are being treated by school authorities and whether students' rights are being respected.

These high school students in California, with support from the ACLU, filed a free speech lawsuit against their high school district to stop their principal from censoring articles on homosexuality in the student newspaper. They won their case.

- Find out what a school's written policy is regarding searching students, conducting drug tests, or disclosing information. Not all schools have written policies, but many states require school districts to write policies regarding student discipline. Students may find that their school violates its own rules or school district rules. Even if no rules are being violated, understanding what the existing rules are can be helpful. Students might be able to suggest changes to the rules that would better protect their rights.

- Contact a local ACLU office if you believe that the school is improperly invading students' right to privacy. Its lawyers could take legal action. At the very least, they can give advice on what students' rights are and whether the school is doing anything legally wrong. The ACLU's lawyers may offer ideas about other ways to help students defend their rights, like suggesting new school district rules on privacy or new school policies.

- Talk to students about having a speaker from the ACLU or another privacy rights group come to speak to students at an assembly or meeting. Students will have a chance to learn more about privacy rights and ask questions in person about their rights.

Challenging a school's policies regarding privacy rights for students can seem daunting. But if you and other students work toward change in a constructive manner, change may actually be instituted.

THE DEBATE OVER
PRIVACY RIGHTS

T he Fourth Amendment creates a right to be free from government searches, but privacy exists in other areas, too. The Supreme Court very slowly recognized a specific right to privacy in the Constitution. Today, Americans have a constitutional right to privacy, but it is still unclear exactly what their constitutional privacy rights include.

The Court has said that the constitutional right to privacy includes rights related to controlling the human body, especially regarding contraception and abortion. Sex and intimacy are certainly among the things that Americans—and people in most other cultures—keep most private. The most controversial privacy decisions deal with a right to abortion. Certainly, abortion affects the private lives of women in serious ways.

The issue of abortion is controversial because people have personal opinions about the subject. Some people think abortion involves a private decision about whether or not to bear children and that the government should not be able to interfere with that decision. Others think that abortion is not a private matter because it involves ending a human life, something a woman should not be permitted to do. The questions are: What constitutes a private matter? What constitutes an issue that the public or the government should become involved in?

Think about whether the right to privacy as protected by the Constitution should be more narrowly or more widely defined. The Constitution is the supreme law of the United States. Should the courts be very careful about creating a right where none existed before because constitutional rights create such serious limits on the ability of Congress and the states to pass laws that conflict with those rights? Moreover, privacy is never mentioned in the Constitution, so perhaps a court should follow the Constitution's text to the letter and not protect privacy at all. On the other hand, Americans have seen how the people who wrote the Constitution cared about privacy, whether it meant protection from unreasonable searches and seizures or from troops quartered in people's homes. Perhaps the job of the courts is to protect individuals' rights and make sure that the Constitution adapts to the problems and needs of today? Think about the role of the courts as you read about the Supreme Court's privacy decisions. These decisions are some of the most controversial and exciting cases that the Court has ever decided. They raise many interesting

A couple speaks with a doctor about pregnancy issues. Currently, U.S. laws protect the privacy rights of women in the United States who wish to use contraception or have an abortion.

questions about rights and what the job of the Supreme Court should be.

The first case to recognize a constitutional right to privacy is the renowned case of *Griswold v. Connecticut*, decided in 1965. (Remember, courts had already recognized a common law right to privacy, mostly a right not to have people use your image or appearance in print, or to release your personal information.) The *Griswold* case was brought by Planned Parenthood of Connecticut, a group that was protesting laws that prevented women from getting abortions or using contraceptives. Planned Parenthood hoped to challenge the law that prevented anyone from selling contraceptives and asked a Connecticut doctor to help it distribute contraceptives and counsel couples in the use of contraceptives. The doctor and an official at the Planned Parenthood office were both sued and fined $100. The lawyers for Planned Parenthood argued that the doctor could not be punished because the law violated the right to patient privacy. They argued that married couples should be able to decide if they want to use contraception and that their decisions about whether or not to have children are very private decisions that the government cannot interfere with. The government cannot regulate family size, they said.

Justice William O. Douglas wrote the Supreme Court decision. He said that although the word "privacy" never appears in the Constitution, the right is "implied" in the Bill of Rights. The Bill of Rights already protects against several different kinds of unreasonable government actions that interfere with our private lives. We have discussed the Fourth Amendment, which prohibits police from making unreasonable searches. The Third Amendment was discussed in *Griswold*, which was really the first time that the Supreme Court had ever addressed it. The Third Amendment's text protects against quartering troops in people's homes. However, the Court said that the amendment also embodies the general idea that people's homes should be protected from unreasonable intrusions. The Third Amendment is concerned with privacy, the Court said.

Justice Douglas said that privacy is one of our "fundamental rights." "Fundamental right" would become the term the Supreme Court would always come to use to refer to rights like the right to privacy, which are important rights even though they are not in the actual text of the Constitution. Justice Douglas suggested that the right to privacy comes from "penumbras" of the Bill of Rights. Penumbras are the lighter edges of shadows. A penumbra of the Bill of Rights would be a kind of shadow, or background, of the Bill of Rights. Justice Douglas's use of the word "penumbras" was very new and confusing at the time. Many people still wonder what he meant. What the idea of penumbras really implies is that the right to privacy is in the background whenever people talk about other parts of the Bill of Rights, like the right to be safe from the police or to be safe from certain kinds of intrusions. The general right to privacy is not named in the Bill of Rights, but it is the purpose behind some of the specific rights that are listed therein.

Specifically, Justice Douglas argued that the right to privacy is among the rights that are given to the people by the Ninth Amendment. When the Framers wrote the Bill of Rights, they did not want to give the impression that the list of rights in it included all of the rights that people should have. The Bill of Rights includes only the ones that they thought were important to list. So the Ninth Amendment says, "The enumeration in the Constitution of certain rights shall not be construed to deny or disparage others retained by the people." What does it mean for the people to retain rights? Can a court just arbitrarily decide that people have a right to something and strike down whatever state law it pleases? If this were the case, and if a court decided that drivers have a right to speed, for instance, courts could strike down speed limits. There must be some standard that decides which unnamed rights are part of the Bill of Rights and which are not. Justice Douglas thought that because the right to privacy was so important, it was obvious that it should be included under the Bill of Rights. He said that "a relationship lying within the zone of privacy [is] a right older than the Bill of Rights." In other words, it is argued that the right to privacy is so old and basic that it is an essential part of other rights that are listed in the Bill of Rights, so the Court must protect it.

Even if it is true that there is a very basic, though unwritten, right to privacy in the Bill of Rights, what does a right to privacy have to do with adults buying contraceptives? The Supreme Court seemed worried about the idea that the government might search people's homes to find out if they were using contraceptives. In later cases, the Court also emphasized that decisions about whether to have a child or not are life-changing decisions that the government should not make for us. But does the Court's ruling that many decisions are personal mean that the government is obligated to let children buy contraceptives or allow contraceptives to be given out in schools?

Not all of the judges agreed that recognizing a right to privacy was a good idea. Supreme Court Justice Hugo Black disagreed with the Court's decision. He disagreed with the idea of privacy rights and always argued that the Court should not recognize any rights that are not part of the actual text of the Constitution. He dissented in *Griswold*, which means that he wrote a separate opinion from the decision of the majority of the judges to express why he disagreed with the majority. He wrote, "I like my privacy as well as the next one, but I am nevertheless compelled to admit that government has a right to invade it unless prohibited by some specific constitutional provision." Many people still think that because the right is never mentioned in the Constitution, there should not be a constitutional right to privacy. Instead, they think Americans should rely on protections in laws that Congress and the states pass or on the rights in the common law mentioned earlier.

For twenty years after *Griswold*, the Supreme Court developed the idea of a right to privacy and soon expanded the right to protect privacy in three areas of private life: childbearing, including the right to abortion and contraception; marriage, including the striking down of antimiscegenation laws (laws that stated that people of different races could not marry) and divorce restrictions; and education of children.

Why these areas? Laws affecting these vital areas of people's lives "tend to take over the lives of the persons involved, they direct a life's development along a particular avenue," wrote Jed Rubenfield in "The Right of Privacy" (102 *Harvard Law Review* 737 [1989]). Reproduction, marriage, and education all involve important family decisions that change a person's life, and if the government could control these decisions, people would have very little freedom.

Yet, the government does make decisions that limit privacy, even in these special areas relating to sex and reproduction. Marriage is controlled by many kinds of laws that decide what a legal marriage consists of. Most state laws prohibit the marriage of gay couples, other laws state that couples must be of a certain age to marry, and they must fill out certain forms and have a certain kind of official present. Once married, special tax rules apply to the couple. Education also has many restrictions—families must send children to public schools unless they can show that their children are educated privately. As in other areas, privacy rights are always balanced between public interests and private interests.

Cases after *Griswold* often involved childbearing issues. In 1972, in *Eisenstadt v. Baird*, the Supreme Court overturned a law that made it a crime to distribute contraceptives to unmarried people. The Court said, "If the right of privacy means anything, it is the right of the individual, married or single, to be free from unwarranted government intrusion into matters so fundamentally affecting a person as the decision whether to bear or beget a child."

Five years later, in *Carey v. Population Services International*, the Court struck down a New York law that prohibited the sale of contraceptives to minors under the age of sixteen. The privacy right applies to all people, not just adults.

These decisions helped develop the idea of a constitutional right to privacy. The Supreme Court held that the right comes from the due process clause of the Fourteenth Amendment. The idea that the due process clause restricts things that government can do is called substantive due process.

ABORTION RIGHTS

These right-to-privacy cases culminated in 1973 in *Roe v. Wade* and its companion case, *Doe v. Bolton*. In 1970, a pregnant and single woman using the

Pro-choice activists rally in Washington, D.C., while an abortion rights case is being heard at the U.S. Supreme Court. The Court's 1973 ruling in *Roe v. Wade* continues to be very controversial.

pseudonym Jane Roe sued in federal court in Dallas, Texas. She challenged a Texas law that prohibited abortion and made it a crime except when "procured or attempted by medical advice for the purpose of saving the life of the mother." The case eventually went to the Supreme Court.

The Supreme Court ruled that women have a fundamental right to receive abortions, overturning laws in all fifty states that restricted access to abortion. *Roe v. Wade* is one of the most controversial Supreme Court decisions ever, and it is certainly the most well-known decision concerning a right to privacy. The Court held that a woman's right to privacy is a "fundamental right" under the Fourteenth Amendment. The reasoning that led the Court to this decision was complex.

One thing the Supreme Court did to reach its 1973 decision was to review the history of the laws that made abortion illegal. It said that these laws were very new and that abortion had actually been legal throughout most of the nation's history. In colonial times, abortions were commonly practiced, and abortion had remained legal throughout the United States until the end of the nineteenth century.

By the 1960s, however, abortion had for many years been declared illegal everywhere in the United States, although some doctors still performed the procedure and some citizen groups were asking that it be legalized. In the 1960s, this movement to legalize abortion spread nationwide. During those years, advocates of legal abortion received increased support because of the tragic birth defects caused by the pregnancy drug thalidomide. Sherri Finkbine, an Arizona television personality, had taken the drug during her pregnancy and was told that her baby would be born severely deformed and that an abortion would be necessary. Arizona required three doctors to approve the abortion, and Finkbine spoke to the press about her story, hoping to help other women avoid birth defects. But when her story gained national media attention, her doctors canceled her abortion because they feared they might be prosecuted as criminals under Arizona's abortion law.

Finkbine ended up having to obtain an abortion in Sweden. Less wealthy women who wanted an abortion could not even afford to be treated by a real doctor, much less travel all the way to Europe. Since abortion was illegal in the United States, many of the people who were offering abortions, especially to women who were poor, were incompetent or not even doctors at all. Real doctors who were qualified to do abortions often feared that they would lose their licenses if it became known that they were performing them. As a result, thousands of women died each year from botched operations or from the unsafe or unsanitary practices used by "back alley" abortionists. *Roe v. Wade* was decided at the height of the movement to legalize abortion. The Supreme Court said that the right of privacy was "broad enough to encompass a woman's decision whether or not to terminate her pregnancy." This kind of right to privacy may seem more like the freedom to choose than the kind of privacy rights that we have been talking about so far, such as the right to freedom from intrusion or searches. However, a woman's decision about whether or not to reproduce is indeed a very private one. If a state bans abortion, it is making that decision for every woman who lives within its borders, thus making a private decision impossible.

The Supreme Court weighed the value of a woman's free choice and liberty against the life of the fetus. The *Roe v. Wade* decision attempted a delicate balance and was very specific. The decision said that a state cannot ban or even regulate abortions during the first three months of pregnancy, which constitute the first trimester, and went on to say that a state can regulate abortion during the second trimester (the fourth, fifth, and sixth months of pregnancy) only for reasons having to do with protecting the health of the mother. The point at which a woman's right to abortion ends, the Court said, has to do with the precise point in the pregnancy beyond which the fetus should be considered "alive." Traditionally, common law judges thought of a child as truly alive only at the point of "quickening," when the child first begins to kick. In *Roe v. Wade*, the Court ruled that only at the beginning of the third trimester is the fetus viable, meaning that it would be capable of living outside of the mother's womb. So during this third trimester, the last three months of pregnancy, the life of the fetus becomes an issue, and therefore a state is allowed to ban abortion during this late stage of pregnancy. But the Court also said that abortion must always be allowed—no matter

Pro-life activists demonstrate in California on the thirty-third anniversary of the Supreme Court's *Roe v. Wade* decision to legalize abortion.

how far along in her pregnancy a woman is—when that abortion is necessary to preserve the life or health of the mother.

The *Roe v. Wade* decision has been criticized by religious groups that argue a fetus is a person from the moment of conception and that the life of the fetus cannot be sacrificed at any time. (Some religious groups would allow abortion if it is necessary to save the life of the mother.) But the Supreme Court said that the fetus is not a person until the third trimester and so the mother's rights should be weighed more heavily up until that time. This issue is still hotly debated.

In yet another kind of privacy decision, *Frisby v. Schultz* (1988), the Supreme Court held that a town can pass a law saying that protesters must not picket in front of the home of one individual. Large groups of antiabortion protesters had picketed in front of a Wisconsin doctor's home, shouting slogans and calling the doctor a baby killer. The Court said that the privacy of people at home is too important to be ignored and that there are other ways for a group to convey a message without singling out one person's home. The Court said, "There is simply no right to force speech into the home of an unwilling listener."

Some people who support the right to abortion think that the Supreme Court should have reasoned its decision in *Roe v. Wade* differently. Some think that the decision is too specific—it makes the Court seem like it is passing a law, not defining a general kind of right. Others think that the Court should not have based the decision on a right to choose or a privacy right. Instead, they see the abortion debate as really being about sex discrimination: denying women the right to control reproduction invades their bodies and forces them to bear children in a way that the law never forces men. Constitutional law scholar Laurence Tribe argues, "Current law nowhere forces men to sacrifice their bodies and restructure their lives even in those tragic situations (of needed organ transplants, for example) where nothing less will permit their children to survive." If men do not have to give up a kidney to save their born child's life, why should women be forced to bear the hardship of bringing a child to birth to save a child that is not yet born and may not really be alive according to many definitions. Indeed, courts often recognize a right to control one's body, and denying only women that right seems discriminatory.

Other people criticize the decision from a scientific point of view. *Roe* draws a line that places the viability of a fetus at the beginning of the third trimester. After that line, the state can ban abortion. But what if, as a result of the progress of science, a fetus can become viable, or able to survive outside its mother's womb, much earlier in the pregnancy, maybe even from the moment of conception? In that case, would women lose the right to abortion?

AFTER *ROE V. WADE*

The controversy over abortion rights did not end with *Roe*. In 1989, in *Webster v. Reproductive Health Services*, the Supreme Court looked at a Missouri law intended to encourage women to give birth to their children, rather than have abortions. The law banned the use of any public facilities to perform abortions. In areas where most people often used public hospitals, this law might have made abortion services very scarce in large parts of the state. The Court said that the law was permissible, and that states can use their facilities as they see fit. Three justices also argued that *Roe v. Wade* should be overturned.

In recent years, as more conservative justices have been appointed, the Supreme Court has gone on to partially overrule *Roe*. Of course, many people think it's wrong that important constitutional rights should depend on the number of votes a certain point of view can muster in the Supreme Court. Instead, many think that judges should interpret the law only as objectively and fairly as they can, ignoring their own political or moral views. However, for better or for worse, some of the Republican appointments to the Supreme Court were made using abortion as a litmus test—that is, candidates were appointed only if it was clear that they opposed abortion rights and wanted to overrule *Roe*. However, the idea that judges should be impartial has continued because, even with many new appointments, *Roe v. Wade* has managed to survive.

In *Planned Parenthood v. Casey* (1992), the Supreme Court returned to the subject of abortion rights. With five conservative Republican justices on the Court, many feared that *Roe v. Wade* would be overruled; and indeed Justice Scalia argued for over-ruling *Roe* in a dissent. Pennsylvania had passed a law saying that women must wait twenty-four hours after receiving information about abortion before having one. Married women were also required to notify their husbands. These rules were designed to discourage women from having abortions without actually banning abortions. Many other states were also considering substantial restrictions on access to abortion.

The Supreme Court did not overturn the right to abortion, but it did step away from the reasoning in *Roe*. One reason why the Court did not overturn *Roe* is that it is bound by precedent. This means that courts are supposed to follow past decisions, except under very unusual circumstances. People rely on decisions of a court and want the law to be stable, so courts are reluctant to make dramatic changes in the law. Therefore, in *Planned Parenthood v. Casey*, the Supreme Court followed the precedent but made smaller changes in the law. The Court got rid of the entire trimester framework and instead said more generally that states cannot place "undue burdens" on the right to abortion. The Court also placed more emphasis on how the right to abortion is an important protection against discrimination. Abortion still receives protection as a right, and states cannot forbid all abortions. States now have an easier time, though, passing laws that make abortions more difficult to obtain.

Justice Harry Blackmun, who wrote the decision in *Roe v. Wade*, saw that as more conservative justices joined the Court and support for the decision dwindled, abortion rights were only barely squeaking by. He wrote a defense of *Roe*, saying, "In a Nation that cherishes liberty, the ability of a woman to control the biological operation of her body...must fall within that limited sphere of individual autonomy that lies beyond the will of the power of any transient majority...This Court stands as the ultimate guarantor of that zone of privacy."

In 2003, the Partial-Birth Abortion Ban Act was enacted. The law prohibits abortion in cases where the fetus has started to make its way out of the birth canal. The law states, "Any physician who, in or affecting interstate or foreign commerce, knowingly performs a partial-birth abortion and thereby kills a human fetus shall be fined under this title or imprisoned not more than two years, or both." In 2007, the law was challenged and the Supreme Court upheld it. Even in cases where the physician feels the mother's life is at risk, late-term abortions were outlawed in all states.

Minors and Abortion

In a 1976 case called *Planned Parenthood of Missouri v. Danforth*, the Supreme Court said that states cannot pass laws that let parents prevent their children who are minors from having abortions. More recently, the Court has permitted some kinds of parental consent laws that do not give parents a veto but still make it much more difficult for young people to obtain abortions.

The Supreme Court in *Planned Parenthood v. Casey* upheld a Pennsylvania parental consent rule that says an unemancipated minor cannot obtain an abortion unless she and one of her parents provide consent. "Emancipated" means that the woman is sufficiently mature or independent enough to make the decision on her own; a judge can make the decision about whether or not a woman is an emancipated minor. The law allows a "judicial bypass" option whereby the woman can ask a judge for special permission to have an abortion without telling her parents. This law even requires that the parent must listen to alternatives to abortion and receive state literature encouraging him or her to make his or her daughter have the baby. This law makes having an abortion especially difficult for minors, and many states have enacted similar laws. Other laws, called squeal rules, require doctors to tell the parents of a minor about a proposed abortion.

Is the Supreme Court letting states violate privacy rights by forcing young mothers to have unwanted children? Giving parents veto power gives them control over the lives of their children. Do these state laws encourage more teen pregnancies, which hurt teenage women without affecting young men? Are these laws a form of sex discrimination because they seriously affect the lives of women? Or do they just reflect different schools of thought regarding the life of the unborn so that states should be able to target young women in this way, despite the rights involved?

If you want to learn about any restrictions on abortion in your state, there are many abortion rights groups that you can contact. Planned Parenthood has chapters and clinics in most states. It can offer abortion counseling, as well as volunteer opportunities.

THE RIGHT TO MARRY

The Supreme Court has said that the right to marry is a fundamental one. Deciding to get married is one of the most important decisions that people make. It is like the decision to have a child—it changes people's lives for many years to come. Marriage is also an important cultural institution, and for many people it is treated as a sacred and momentous event in a couple's life. Marriage seems like an important kind of privacy right. Marriage also brings with it many privileges, like tax privileges, joint ownership, and the right to see a spouse in the hospital. Denying some people the chance to marry denies them privileges, and it can make them seem like less than real citizens.

Remember, the South did not permit black slaves to marry. This meant that they did not have the chance to make their relationships legal, to have the law recognize that a couple was bound together. One of the reasons why the equal protection clause was passed was to make sure that blacks would be able to marry. Southern states continued to use marriage laws to try to make blacks second-class citizens even after the Civil War and the passage of the Fourteenth Amendment. As recently as the 1960s, more than twenty states prevented people of different races from marrying. These racist laws, called antimiscegenation laws, were often explicitly passed to protect "the purity of the white race" and enforce a society segregated by race. The Supreme Court, in *Loving v. Virginia* in 1967, held that states cannot prevent couples from marrying because of race. The Court said that a law that tries to do so violates the equal protection clause because it discriminates by race. It also stated that marriage is a "fundamental right," or a privacy right.

The Supreme Court has said that marriage cannot be denied to people just because they are poor. Many times, unfortunately, the ability to exercise a right can depend on whether or not you have money. And sometimes, the courts decide that being denied a right because you lack money is too unfair to be permitted. In the 1978 case *Zablocki v. Redhail*, the Supreme Court struck down a Wisconsin law that said residents of Wisconsin could not marry if they owed any child support money. The law meant that poorer people who could not afford to pay child support could never marry. The Court argued that marriage is such a fundamental part of freedom that the government cannot pass laws that make it difficult or impossible for people to marry just because they are poor. In the same way, states cannot make it difficult for poor people to receive divorces and require large fees to obtain divorces.

There is an important debate in the country today about one group of people who are still not permitted to marry in most states. Gay and lesbian partners are only permitted to marry in Massachusetts, Connecticut, Iowa, Vermont, New Hampshire, and the District of Columbia, even though there are many gay couples in all states that have long relationships, adopt children, and lead their lives in the same way that married heterosexual couples do.

Marriage involves many financial benefits—married couples are given reduced taxes and other special benefits. Gay and lesbian couples cannot receive these benefits in most states. Even in cases where same-sex couples live together and run a household together with children, their state may not recognize their union or give them the same benefits as families with a man and a woman as parents.

THE FIGHT FOR SAME-SEX MARRIAGE RIGHTS

Rights protection for gays and lesbians is a relatively new issue in the United States. It was not until 2003 that sexual acts between people of the same sex became legal nationwide. The Supreme Court had not been supportive of gay rights. The Court has said in its 1986 decision in *Bowers v. Hardwick* that states are allowed to make homosexuality a criminal offense. It stated that "the Court is most vulnerable and it comes nearest to illegitimacy" if it recognizes new rights. The majority opinion also said that if the Court recognized a right to engage in homosexual activity, a "parade of horrible" would come next, and the Court would have to say that other sexual activity is acceptable, too, like "adultery, incest, and other sexual crimes." The Court was not sure where to draw

Supporters of same-sex marriage march in San Francisco, California, after the state supreme court upheld Proposition 8, a voter-approved ban on same-sex marriage, in May 2009.

the line and emphasized that many states traditionally had laws against homosexual activity.

Discrimination against gays and lesbians was common for many years, and the Supreme Court didn't do much to protect their rights. It was not until 1996 that the Court did make a more supportive decision in a case called *Romer v. Evans*. Colorado had passed a very unusual kind of law that said that gays and lesbians could not be protected by antidiscrimination laws.

Any other kind of group could be protected, but not gays and lesbians. The Court struck down the law, saying that the state could not single out gays and lesbians for disfavored treatment.

The issue of same-sex marriage has been extremely controversial. California began allowing same-sex marriage in 2008 based on a ruling of the State Supreme Court. But just five months later, an amendment called Proposition 8 was added to California's state constitution. Prop 8 stated that marriage could only be between a man and a woman. In August 2010, a judge declared that the ban on gay marriages was unconstitutional, but stayed his order almost immediately. Staying his order means that his declaration was temporarily suspended and same-sex marriages are still not permitted. The state has gone back and forth about the topic and may continue to do so for some time.

In October 2010, according to the Associated Press, the U.S. Justice Department defended the federal law that defines marriage as between a man and a woman by appealing two rulings in Massachusetts by a judge who called the law unconstitutional for denying federal benefits to same-sex married couples. President Barack Obama has stated repeatedly that he would like to see the law, the 1996 Defense of Marriage Act, be repealed. However, the Justice Department has defended the constitutionality of the act, which it is required to defend.

PRIVACY AND THE CONSTITUTION

Privacy is a right under the Constitution, but only in the three areas just discussed: childbearing (abortion and contraception), marriage (miscegenation and divorce restrictions), and education of children. All of these involve very important issues, but Americans usually think of the right to privacy as being much larger, including areas such as protecting the privacy of conversations from eavesdroppers and being free from police searches.

Some people think that because the Constitution is the supreme law of the land, courts should be very hesitant to create any new interpretations of it. They think that the courts should have a very limited role and only follow the literal text of the document. The idea that there can be no rights in the Constitution that are not specifically written down is called textualism. While many people think that the text of the Constitution is very important, almost no lawyer thinks that the text is enough on its own. One problem is that the words "a constitutional right to privacy" are very vague much of the time and seem like they were intended to be interpreted by the courts. For example, the courts have to decide what an "unreasonable search" is because the Fourth Amendment does not list all of the things that police

DON'T ASK, DON'T TELL

For many years, the U.S. military had a long-standing policy in which gays were forbidden to serve in any of the branches of the armed forces. Over time, discrimination lawsuits were being filed against the military, and people were becoming sensitive to the issue of gays in the military. Many servicemen, servicewomen, and training personnel thought that they would feel uncomfortable serving with homosexual comrades. They had to live so closely together with them and work alongside them in stressful training and combat situations.

To remedy the growing problem, President Bill Clinton issued a policy in 1993 called "Don't Ask, Don't Tell." It stated that the military would not be able to ask someone if he or she was homosexual, and military personnel would not reveal the person's sexual orientation. The argument was that the issue of someone's sexual orientation was a private one and should not be a factor in the person's military career. In reality, the policy was a ban on openly gay personnel in the military.

The policy worked for many years. Then people began to question if it was fair to ask gays to hide their sexual orientation and forbid them from discussing it. In any other career, it was not forbidden to be openly gay. The argument was that people today are less threatened by homosexuality than they were years ago when the "Don't Ask, Don't Tell" policy was put into place. In September 2010, a federal judge in California decided that a ban on openly gay service members violates the U.S. Constitution. Then in October 2010, the same judge ordered the U.S. military to stop enforcing the policy. According to the *New York Times*, the judge wrote that the policy "infringes the fundamental rights of U.S. service

members and prospective service members" and violates their rights of due process and freedom of speech. Then, on December 18, 2010, Congress passed legislation repealing the policy. President Barack Obama signed the legislation four days later. Before the law can be put into effect, the Secretary of Defense and the Chairman of the Joint Chiefs of Staff must certify that changing the law will not harm U.S. military readiness.

can or cannot do—all it provides is a short declaration of a right.

Other people think that Americans have to read meaning into the Constitution, but that they should follow the intent of the people who wrote it. People who care most about the original intent of the Constitution are often called originalists. Supreme Court Justices Antonin Scalia and Clarence Thomas are probably the most well known originalists. One big problem is that not only are the words in the Constitution unclear, but we often know very little about the intent of the people who wrote the document. The Fourteenth Amendment, which was enacted after the Civil War, is in some ways just as important as the original Bill of Rights, since the amendment made rights apply against the states. All of these privacy decisions are about things that states have done to restrict abortion or marriage. So should the intent of the authors of the Fourteenth Amendment be what really matters? And why should Americans care about intent? What if their intent was that Americans should decide for themselves what their rights are?

Other people think that the Constitution was intended to be understood in changing ways over the years. These people believe that the law should be adapted to new ideas and new problems in society. They argue that privacy is an idea that changes over the years. Privacy is a more important right today because there are so many new ways that it can be infringed upon. It was not much of a concern when the government was very small and people led their own lives. Today, the government is very involved in people's lives, and people's lives are also more connected to one another, especially through technology. The people who wrote the Bill of Rights could not have imagined all of the new technological or political problems that would arise. Maybe they would have wanted the courts to adapt to new situations by recognizing new rights or extending old rights into new areas.

These debates over how to interpret the constitutional right to privacy are very important. They reflect the same kinds of issues that the courts themselves are always forced to deal with when interpreting the Constitution.

Just because the U.S. Constitution does not protect everything that Americans think of when they think of privacy does not mean that they do not have a right to privacy. Courts have decided that a right to privacy exists in common law. Many states also protect a right of privacy in their constitutions. Moreover, there are state and federal laws that protect different kinds of privacy rights. Many of the most exciting new areas in privacy law have to do with state or federal legislation and not rights as interpreted by the courts.

MILITARY PROTESTERS, FREE SPEECH, AND PRIVACY RIGHTS

Are religious groups that protest at a military funeral protected by the First Amendment? Or do they violate the right to privacy? A Topeka, Kansas, fundamentalist church argued before the Supreme Court in October 2010 that the church group's carrying of offensive signs and protests outside military funerals are protected by free speech under the First Amendment. According to ABC News, the church's lawyer, who is also the daughter of the church's pastor, told the Supreme Court that her group pickets military funerals with "great circumspection and awareness of boundaries" when it carries signs with messages such as "God Hates You." (The church group expressed its view that U.S. deaths in Afghanistan and Iraq are

Members of the Westboro Baptist Church of Topeka, Kansas, protest in Kentucky at a memorial service for soldiers who were killed in the Iraq War. The Supreme Court ruled for the church on the free-speech case.

God's punishment for American immorality and tolerance of gays and abortion.) She also said that the group files permits with law enforcement authorities before every protest. This particular case involved a U.S. Marine who died in Iraq during the war. The father of the marine sued the church group whose members picketed the funeral, and he won a judgment of $5 million. The ruling, however, was thrown out by a federal appeals court. The federal appeals court said that the protests were not aimed at the father and that the statements are protected by the Constitution's guarantee of free speech because they included "imaginative and hyperbolic rhetoric" that was meant to incite debate.

The father's lawyers argued before the Supreme Court, requesting that the monetary award be reinstated. "We are talking about a funeral," he argued. "If context was ever going to matter, it has to matter for a funeral." A law professor at George Washington University Law School told ABC News, "This case might not have huge constitutional dimensions, but it does raise this very important question, namely: how much protection do relatively private figures have against hurtful, outrageous, insulting, emotionally aggravating speech?" The Court ruled on the case in March 2011, deciding that the First Amendment protects the church members' rights.

Forty U.S. states have passed laws that regulate protests at funerals. ABC News reported in October 2010 that Attorney General Steve Six of Kansas said in defense of the marine's father's case, "The states should be accorded their traditionally recognized police powers to adopt and enforce reasonable time, place, and manner regulations on activities that may disrupt funerals, and to define civil tort [a wrongful act involving injury to persons, property, or reputation, but excluding breach of contract] liability for conduct that intentionally inflicts emotional distress and invades sacred privacy interests." On behalf of the church, the ACLU filed court papers, writing, "First Amendment guarantees of freedom of speech and the free exercise of religion are designed to protect the right of speakers to voice their views on matters of public concern and to express their religious convictions."

States and the Protection of Privacy

Many state constitutions provide greater protections for privacy than the U.S. Constitution does. A state's constitution is the highest law of that state. It gives its citizens rights in the same way that the U.S. Constitution does. Although many people focus on the U.S. Constitution, the United States has, in many ways, fifty constitutions and fifty legal systems. State laws can often provide stronger protection for many rights. States have their own constitutions, their own laws, and their own courts, which decide cases that deal with state laws. If a person's privacy is violated in a state that guarantees a right to privacy, that person may be able to have state courts take action even though federal courts cannot.

Some state constitutions explicitly mention the right to privacy, which—as already noted—the U.S. Constitution does not mention. In one example, voters amended Article 1, Section 1 of the California Constitution in 1972. It now says:

> All people are by nature free and independent and have inalienable rights. Among these are enjoying and defending and liberty, acquiring, possessing, and protecting proper pursuing and obtaining safety, happiness, and privacy.

Nine other state constitutions also guarantee a right to privacy. Of course, courts must still decide what the right to privacy means. Privacy means different things to different people and can involve anything from protection from police searches and surveillance to abortion and marriage rights.

PRIVACY ISSUES TODAY

I ssues of privacy violations are in the news almost every day. People are constantly suggesting new laws to protect privacy because technology is changing so rapidly that it is becoming harder to remain anonymous in today's high-tech world. People trust that some of their most private information will be safe online, such as their bank information and Social Security numbers. Many of Americans' privacy rights are not in the Constitution at all, but exist because lawmakers decided to protect citizens' privacy by passing laws. Because courts have been very reluctant to expand constitutional protections for privacy, many people concerned about the right to privacy are encouraging legislators in Congress and in state legislatures to pass new laws to protect privacy.

Technology is providing people with so many new ways to live their lives, but it is also exposing their lives to new threats. For example, computers make it possible for people to shop and chat online, but they also allow hackers to pry into conversations and find out important personal information. More and more companies are buying private information about individuals so that they can send them catalogs and product information that they think those people want. But this same information can be purchased or obtained by criminals. New technology may allow doctors to find out more about people's health, but people may not find it desirable that anyone with a computer is able to access that kind of private information. The popular social networking site Facebook allows users to connect with hundreds of friends at once, but it also periodically changes its policies about how much information can be revealed about individuals without their permission. It is even possible for someone to know your exact location through Facebook. Users must be savvy enough to know how to protect themselves amid these constantly changing policies.

EVERYDAY SURVEILLANCE

In the last few years, many cities and neighborhoods have vastly increased the use of video surveillance cameras. The New York Civil Liberties Union recently published a map of downtown Manhattan with pins showing where video surveillance cameras are installed. The map was covered with pins; it is hard to walk anywhere in that area without encountering some kind of security camera. The New York Civil Liberties Union found that on a typical short walk through downtown New York, a person appears on twenty different cameras. This number does not include cameras in stores.

Many of the new cameras are not private cameras owned by stores or security firms. They are owned by the government and monitored by the police. Police find that they are an inexpensive way to watch parks or secluded areas when no officers are around. The video cameras are monitored on a television screen in a central office, and the tapes are usually saved for a few weeks in case a crime is reported near one of them.

The cameras have sometimes been shown to be effective in reducing crime (at least in the area in front of the camera). But many people who are advocates for civil liberties are uncomfortable with all these cameras being everywhere. They do not like the idea of the government watching individuals' every move. Remembering the things that J. Edgar Hoover did while directing the FBI, they wonder what would happen if the wrong kinds of police or authorities took control of all this electronic equipment that watches over us.

The USA PATRIOT Act gives the federal government the power of surveillance to help law enforcement agents catch potential terrorists before they can act. These powers include roving surveillance to track possible terrorists who keep switching cell phones or use other electronic technologies. The government claims that the expansion of such powers is warranted solely because it is the most efficient way for uncovering terrorist plots before they can be carried out.

The opponents to this expansion of power in the PATRIOT Act believe that giving the government unbridled control would mean that law enforcement agencies would engage in widespread spying on typical Americans for the foreseeable future. Questions about whether or not constitutional protections and privacy rights should be upheld during America's war on terror will continue to be asked and debated.

PRIVACY AND TECHNOLOGY

Sometimes, it seems like people have no electronic privacy at all. Phone numbers are displayed to people before they even pick up the phone. Cell phones can easily be tracked in an effort to find them. These are conveniences of the modern world. But when these technologies were first introduced, they were considered invasions of privacy. Americans know that the authorities have the ability to track their activities electronically. Yet, while federal authorities have been given permission to tap phones under certain situations, federal law does not permit private citizens to listen to one another's phone conversations. The rules seem to be in favor of the authorities, rather than the average citizen. If you secretly tape a phone conversation, you might be breaking the law. People have been fired or passed over for jobs because employers did not like something they read on their Facebook page or other networking site. At the same time, these people would not be permitted to monitor the site of the prospective employer.

Many electronic privacy laws have not been updated or revised since the 1990s, before cell phones and other such technology became mainstream.

PERSONAL INFORMATION ONLINE

In many ways, electronic surveillance is more troubling than a physical search because you rarely know that it is even occurring. Taping phone conversations is old technology, and new computer technology is much more powerful and threatening to privacy rights. Justice Brandeis feared long ago that numerous mechanical devices would threaten to make good the prediction that "what is whispered in the closet shall be proclaimed from the housetops." The Internet has created an entire new virtual world in which the walls and neighborhoods and physical space that protect our privacy have no meaning. Computer networks manage so much information, make information so easy to access, and can store information in so many different places that the Internet provides huge new opportunities for others to access personal information about you that you never even knew existed. The Internet connects computers to each other, giving experienced hackers access to private information in

A teen uses Facebook as a social networking site. Facebook has guides to help users secure their profile pages, account settings, privacy settings, and location settings.

other people's computers. Millions of e-mail messages are sent every day. On the Internet, they travel through many computers before they reach their final destinations. Very few of the messages sent over the Internet are secure. By "sniffing" computers along the way, other people can read your e-mail as it travels to its destination.

Facebook presents particular privacy challenges to millions of people worldwide. You may have hundreds of friends, and simply clicking that you "like" something that a friend writes can reveal your identity to countless other people and your connection to that person. If privacy settings are not set to the highest level, you may be either giving out information about yourself or even revealing lists of your personal connections to companies, hackers, and others. You can even risk the privacy of others without their permission. Posting pictures of a party can reveal information about you, your whereabouts, and your personal connections to others. You may be putting an image of someone else online who does not approve of his or her image being used. That person may choose not to be on Facebook because of concern over privacy issues. But posting pictures of that person does not require permission, and the photo can instantly be seen by hundreds of your friends and possibly a network of hundreds of your friends' friends.

According to Computerworld.com in October 2010, Facebook created new tools to give users more control over their personal information. One feature is designed to enable users to download any of their information from the site, another allows users to monitor which applications they have used on the social networking site and delete them easily. Another feature allows users to split up their friends into subgroups so that they can make certain posts available for only a particular group of online friends to view. The new tools were created in response to an outcry over Facebook's privacy issues and control of personal information by users.

If you ever want to see how much information an Internet site can instantly obtain about your computer, visit http://www.Privacy.net/analyze. This site instantly lists information about the sites you have recently visited, what kind of computer you own, what kind of Internet service you use, and who owns your Internet provider. If that is just the information that can immediately be obtained from your computer, think of what determined hackers could do to access credit card numbers or more personal information.

President Clinton proposed a "global information infrastructure" that would have some protections for privacy on the Internet. Today, there is a commission to address global information infrastructure, but the commission is not active in lawmaking or setting policies. It meets to discuss the current challenges of Internet privacy.

Many lawmakers think that increasing personal privacy is too daunting a task to tackle on the Internet. Some Web sites do provide information on privacy on the Internet. A group of sites have a program called eTrust, which rates sites based on their ability to protect the privacy of users. Technology for protecting privacy and ensuring that messages are secure on the Internet is always changing. And new technology is constantly being cracked by hackers trying to prove their skills, show weakness in protections, or do damage to sites and obtain personal information. Hackers

have made a business out of stealing credit card numbers over the Internet, for example.

One way to keep e-mail secure is to use encryption software, which codes messages and then encodes them again when they reach their destination. Most important to Internet commerce, encryption programs protect credit card numbers when people make purchases over the Internet. Of course, even the most advanced encryption codes have been broken by hackers.

These teens are using a free Wi-Fi hot spot to access the Internet outdoors. Always secure personal information on your computer by ensuring that the proper privacy settings have been activated before you use it in the open.

Today, people's privacy is extremely vulnerable online. Insecure connections can allow users to be hacked easily. When a person goes into a public place and taps into a free Wi-Fi hotspot, the connection does not provide security. The person's computer must have the privacy settings already in place before going to that public area. People do not have to live in constant fear of their computers being hacked, but they must protect their computers in public just as they would protect their other personal belongings.

New Internet sites create new personal information that most people never knew they had. A department store may keep records of what you buy in order to study consumer tastes. Many Web sites also track the things that you look at. One Internet company was sued because the software that it gave away to play music on secretly sent information back to the software maker, telling it what kinds of music people preferred.

In October 2010, the *New York Times* reported that Web developers in the coming years will have the capability to give marketers and advertisers access to many more specifics about computer users' online habits and activities. A new Web code, called HTML 5, will help bring in a new era of Internet browsing, making it easier for people to view multimedia content without having to obtain additional software, check their e-mail messages while offline, and find a restaurant or make purchases on a smartphone. The new code will present more tracking opportunities that can be collected and stored in a user's hard drive (some call it a supercookie) while the user is online. Some technology experts believe that weeks or perhaps months of personal data could then be viewed by advertisers. Some of this information could include a user's location, photographs, blog texts, contents of shopping carts and e-mails, and even the user's history of Web browsing. One privacy proponent stated that the new Web code "opens Pandora's box of tracking in the Internet."

There have been many class-action lawsuits charging large media companies and some technology companies with violating users' right to privacy by tracking their online movements even after the users took steps to stop it. The majority of users control their online privacy by changing the settings in their Web browsers. However, each browser has specific privacy settings, and deleting such data can be challenging for most people. Many technology experts and software developers argue that as technology progresses, users have to balance the technological advances of devices and communications with their ability to control their privacy.

Privacy rights conflict with public interests on the Internet just like in the other areas that have been mentioned. With new technology, the government wants to assert its "public interest" in monitoring Americans' lives.

The Federal Trade Commission (FTC) works to protect people against privacy issues on the Internet, including identity theft and protection against spyware. Spyware is software that is installed on a person's computer without his or her knowledge. The software tracks the person's movements on the computer, including Web sites visited and even keystrokes entered. This can translate into passwords being stolen or identities being threatened or stolen.

A person who has had his or her identity stolen has an extremely difficult time proving to authorities that the theft actually took place. If accounts are open in someone's name, loans are approved in that person's name, and purchases are made in that person's name, it would be very difficult to convince banks, authorities, and credit card companies that the approvals were not actually valid. Some victims of identity theft had to spend years clearing up the problems with authorities.

The Department of Justice includes a division called the Computer Crime and Intellectual Property Section that helps in prosecuting various computer crimes that have affected private and public businesses and their computer systems, including the hacking of phone networks, selling of counterfeit computer parts, theft of trade secrets through economic espionage, stealing of student loan records, selling of fake drugs on the Internet, pirating of software, e-mail spam conspiracies, and more.

HOW SAFE IS YOUR PERSONAL INFORMATION?

It does not take a hacker to invade your privacy over the Internet. A great deal of very personal information can be obtained legally, and this has some people worried. There are data collection companies that obtain private information about people. Why? They want to get lists of people who want to buy certain kinds of products and then sell those lists to other companies. Many of the catalogs and offers that you get in the mail are not things that you asked for; a data collection company somehow found out about you and decided that you might buy something from those catalogs or take advantage of those offers.

Data collection companies are not doing anything illegal. They search information that is publicly available on the Internet. When people sign up for a credit card or order a product, they usually fill out a personal information card. They fill out their Social Security numbers, addresses, and favorite kinds of products, not knowing that this information will be made available or sold to other companies that collect personal information. Some people think that Americans should be warned that if they give out their information, it will be distributed to all of these other people. The law does not yet require any warnings like that, though.

SPYWARE

Spyware can ruin a person's computer by slowing it down or making it crash. The worst part is that nobody ever asks for spyware to be installed. It is often bundled in other software, usually with a trick to get the user to download it. Software packages with children's games can be installed by unsuspecting parents, and a spyware program might automatically be installed with them, tracking the users' online activity. This gives the spyware distributor information about what to advertise to users, and it can collect personal information as well. Windows computers that run Explorer Web browsers tend to be most vulnerable, as the software targets these users more. People should be sure that the software they are installing comes from a legitimate source. A firewall can also help prevent spyware from being installed. Checking a computer's security settings and updating software frequently can ensure that the latest protection is available and being used.

Selling information about people is a huge business. Credit companies make large amounts of money storing information about whether people are a credit risk, including information about income, employment, marital status, court records, and past payment of debts and loans. Even Social Security numbers, which are supposed to be personal numbers used for tax collection purposes, are widely available. Companies buy this information and use it to create personal "look up" services, some of which anyone can use right on the Internet.

There is very little legal protection against this kind of personal information use. The 1974 Privacy Act limits some ways that the government can use your information, but it does nothing to prevent these private companies from distributing private information. In contrast, many European countries have very strict rules about distributing private information. The governments in Europe often take a very active role in making sure that no one is giving out people's information and that people are very clearly warned that if they give a company their information, it could be distributed to others. Many people believe that the United States should have stronger laws, too—laws that make giving away personal information illegal and make the government investigate the ways in which companies use personal information.

MEDICAL CONFIDENTIALITY

Medical privacy is another important issue for Americans. The information discussed between a doctor and patient was not always as confidential as it is today. In 2003, a patient privacy act was passed that prevents doctors from discussing a patient's medical records with anyone except the patient, unless prior written permission is given. Doctors are no longer allowed to discuss personal medical information about family members in office waiting rooms where others can overhear. The issue of patient privacy has been thrust into the forefront, and the patient's rights were decided to be most important.

The law also has implications in the workplace. An employer is not allowed to ask about an employee's medical record at any time during the hiring process or at any time the patient works for the company. This keeps companies from discriminating against employees whom they might feel are not healthy enough to do a particular job. Perhaps a diabetic is applying for a job in a grocery store. That issue is not allowed to be discussed or used as a consideration in hiring or firing that person.

Random drug testing is not allowed in most private or public companies. Government employees were required to take mandatory urine tests to determine if they were using drugs. Most state courts no longer allow this type of mandatory testing.

Police can collect genetic information, however. They collect DNA samples from some offenders and can match the samples with evidence at crime sites, just like they do with fingerprints. DNA samples are very accurate and can be taken from something as small as a hair. All fifty states have some kind of DNA database that has information on criminals. For example, New

York's database includes all penal law felons and those convicted of misdemeanors. It also includes DNA information on all people registered as sex offenders. The FBI also has a national DNA database.

Newborn Screening Saves Lives Act

President George W. Bush signed the Newborn Screening Saves Lives Act into law in 2008 to help prevent disease and disability and improve newborn screening methods. The medical intent of the DNA screening of newborns is to increase the number of conditions that can be diagnosed at birth, study the long-term effects of living with the conditions, and develop new medical treatments for the disorders. The law actually establishes a national DNA database. One health care expert and critic of this screening law said in May 2008 that it "imposes a federal agenda of DNA databanking and population-wide genetic research. It does not require consent, and there are no requirements to fully inform parents about the warehousing of their child's DNA for the purpose of genetic research."

In October 2009, the National Institutes of Health (NIH) announced that it was calling its newborn screening research program the Hunter Kelly

Physicians examine DNA sequencing. When a baby is born, blood samples are drawn to test for various illnesses. Some blood spots, however, have been used for additional purposes without the parents' knowledge or consent.

Newborn Screening Research Program within the NIH's Eunice Kennedy Shriver National Institute of Child Health and Human Development division. The name of the screening program is in honor of the son of National Football League Pro Football Hall of

Fame quarterback Jim Kelly. Hunter died of a nervous system disorder at the age of eight. Although many scientists have urged the expansion of the screening program to help benefit medical research so that they can provide treatment and cures for such conditions, there have been some opponents who have raised privacy issues because parents do not give their consent to the research in which their babies' blood spots, or samples, are being used.

According to a report by FOX News in early February 2010, because newborn screening is now mandatory, only a few states provide direct parent education about it. Blood spots that are left over are used to double-check that newborn tests have been performed correctly. In addition, some families ask geneticists to study the spots after a child's death from a disorder that doctors didn't find right away. Scientists, however, have requested to use leftover blood spots for other research, especially those that have been stored for a long time, without contacting parents because the identification of the spots has usually already been deleted. Many people believe there is a good possibility that genetic information about their children could fall into dishonorable hands. Some states, such as Michigan, do have safeguards, stipulating that blood samples can't be subpoenaed for use by law enforcement authorities. Scientists, though, believe that privacy concerns are exaggerated—that medical researchers are after the blood samples, not the babies' names.

In late February 2010, the *Texas Tribune* reported that the Texas Department of State Health Services turned over hundreds of newborn blood samples to the federal government without parental consent to help build a huge "DNA database—a forensics tool designed to identify missing persons and crack cold cases." The *Texas Tribune* revealed that the blood spots were transferred to an armed forces lab to build a national DNA, or perhaps an international, registry. Five parents filed a lawsuit against the state because they believe they were deceived. The state of Texas quickly settled the case. Today, after state lawmakers improved the screening laws, parents in the state receive more information at the hospital about use and storage of blood spots and are presented with an opportunity to opt out of the program. The health services agency in Texas agreed to destroy more than five million blood samples that were collected before the revised legislation took effect.

THE RIGHT TO DIE

One of the most private concerns that a person has is choosing the way he or she wants to die. Maybe the choice of death when one is very ill or in great pain is

Dr. Jack Kevorkian, also called Dr. Death because of his homemade suicide machine that enabled terminally ill patients to end their lives, leaves a county court in Michigan.

a privacy issue, a decision that one wants the "right to be let alone" forever. On the other hand, suicide is a crime, and maybe people should not have the right to have the power of life or death over anyone, including themselves.

Should doctors be allowed to help the terminally ill end their lives? The right to die, as some call it, is partly an issue of technology. New machines can keep people alive for longer and longer, even if their brains are dead. Life support machines keep the heart running, respirators keep the lungs working, and feeding tubes provide nutrients. So the systems of the body are kept functioning. But if the person will never wake from the coma and is basically a "vegetable," should hospitals or families be forced to keep these machines running?

There are ways that people can decide for themselves that they want to die. They have to do it before the fact, though. Courts have said that if people say beforehand that they do not want to be kept alive on these kinds of machines, then that is their choice. People can write documents called living wills, saying that they do not want to be kept alive if they are brain-dead. It is their own private decision, and doctors can then follow their wishes and decide when the time is right to disconnect the machines. Medical charts sometimes have the note "DNR," or "Do Not

Resuscitate." This tells the doctors that a terminally ill patient does not desire to have artificial respirators used to try to bring him or her back to life. But what if a person has not written a living will? Can family members make the decision for their loved one?

What if people are not brain-dead or in a coma? What if they are awake and aware of their surroundings, but in very great pain, perhaps because of a terminal illness? Courts have said that people can commit suicide in certain ways, since they can refuse to take food or medicine. People can "passively" refuse treatment and end their lives that way. But many patients are very weak and therefore request that doctors assist them in ending their lives. This is called physician-assisted suicide. In most states, it is illegal. In the 1980s and 1990s, a doctor named Jack Kevorkian assisted in the suicide of more than forty-five terminally ill patients who requested his help in ending their lives. It was not until 1997 that the Supreme Court decided that physician-assisted suicide was illegal. Kevorkian was sentenced to up to twenty-five years in prison. He was paroled in 2007 at the age of seventy-eight.

The Supreme Court argued that physician-assisted suicide goes against the duties of a doctor. Doctors are required to take an oath that they will do everything they can to protect the lives of their patients (though they cannot force patients to take medication if they refuse). However, people have argued that the courts' prohibition on assisted suicide is wrong. They say that for people who are in a great deal of pain, it is the humane thing to do. Keeping people alive on life support machines is also incredibly expensive. Insurance may not pay for it, and families may not be able to afford it. Families may be bankrupted, or the state may have to pass these costs on to taxpayers. A large percentage of medical costs in America are spent on the last few months of the lives of the elderly.

Should costs matter in cases of life and death? Should the right to die be a private decision for the person and his or her family?

The Court was worried that some suicides might be involuntary, that older patients might be encouraged to commit suicide. However, the Court said only that a law banning assisted suicide was constitutional. It did not say that states cannot permit assisted suicide if they so desire. Physician-assisted suicide is currently permitted in only three states—Oregon, Washington, and Montana—and only under certain circumstances. For example, in Oregon, courts have decided that a doctor may prescribe a lethal dose of medication to a patient who has less than six months to live. However, the doctor cannot be the one to administer the drug, and an agreement must be reached by two doctors that the patient is mentally competent to make the decision to die and that the decision was voluntary.

A technician monitors employees' computers while he works in a server room. Many employers monitor their staff members' Internet use while they are working at the company.

PRIVACY AT WORK

According to a 2007 study, approximately two-thirds of employers monitor their employees' Internet use on the job. More than half of the employers in the study use software that blocks employees from visiting sites that they feel are inappropriate for the workplace. Many companies have fired employees for e-mail or Internet misuse.

While at work, their employers may monitor most people's lives. This monitoring is legal. Most people spend a large percentage of their waking hours at work, so protecting rights at work is especially important. More and more workplaces have video surveillance and systems that can monitor phone conversations and e-mail. Employers use this equipment to watch over employees, fire them, or discipline them for doing anything improper, but also to monitor productivity. Employers argue that they have a right to know what their employees are doing. This kind of monitoring can sometimes be very helpful in protecting the rights of employees. If an employer notices that one employee is sexually harassing another with offensive e-mail messages, the employer can take disciplinary action before the situation becomes even more intolerable to the victim.

Many employers want to conduct background checks before they hire employees. These checks can be quite extensive if the employer wishes them to be. The information allowed in searches varies from state to state. But in many states, it may include a past employment record, criminal records, education history, and personal references. Of course, there is an important legal reason for conducting these tests. Employers can be sued for negligent hiring if they hire someone who has a dangerous history, so they are sometimes required to do these kinds of checks. Day care centers, for example, are required by law in some states to be sure that job applicants are not a danger to children. Here again, there is a trade-off between privacy rights and public safety. Some things that are not allowed to be searched are education records within a particular school, military service records, and medical records.

Employers do not usually need permission to monitor their employees. E-mails, telephones, and even texts from company cell phones are subject to monitoring. Video surveillance in larger companies is allowed and is commonplace. Some employers may state in their employment contracts that all e-mail and voicemail messages are the property of the employer and can be monitored at any time. Many employees, though, do not bother to read the fine print in their contracts or handbooks, so they may not know in advance that they are being listened to or watched.

The lessons to be learned from all of this are not to expect much privacy at work and to be careful not to say or do anything improper on your computer or telephone. Be sure to check your company policy, but it is safer to assume that anything you say or type could be read by a supervisor. Many states have laws that restrict what employers can do in the workplace, but even those laws give employers a great deal of power to monitor employees. If you are fired because of something that your employer has discovered while monitoring a phone call or e-mail, your employer may not even tell you that you were being monitored. Even if your employer does, it may be difficult for you to challenge the decision.

PROTECT YOUR PRIVACY

Although there are more potential breeches in Americans' constitutional right to privacy than ever before, the most important thing that people can do is learn about their rights and how they can protect themselves. Understanding the laws and keeping up with how they change can help protect Americans from having their rights violated. Because the right to privacy is not specifically mentioned in the U.S. Constitution, the Supreme Court's interpretation of it makes a big difference in people's lives. When people know how their rights are defined, they can take actions to protect those rights.

PREAMBLE TO THE CONSTITUTION

We the People of the United States, in order to form a more perfect Union, establish Justice, insure domestic Tranquility, provide for the common defense, promote the general Welfare, and secure the Blessings of Liberty to ourselves and our Posterity, do ordain and establish this Constitution for the United States of America.

On September 25, 1789, Congress transmitted to the state legislatures twelve proposed amendments, two of which, having to do with congressional representation and congressional pay, were not adopted. The remaining ten amendments became the Bill of Rights.

THE BILL OF RIGHTS

Amendment I

Congress shall make no law respecting an establishment of religion, or prohibiting the free exercise thereof; or abridging the freedom of speech, or of the press; or the right of the people peaceably to assemble, and to petition the Government for a redress of grievances.

Amendment II

A well regulated Militia, being necessary to the security of a free State, the right of the people to keep and bear Arms, shall not be infringed.

Amendment III

No Soldier shall, in time of peace be quartered in any house, without the consent of the Owner, nor in time of war, but in a manner to be prescribed by law.

Amendment IV

The right of the people to be secure in their persons, houses, papers, and effects, against unreasonable searches and seizures, shall not be violated, and no Warrants shall issue, but upon probable cause, supported by Oath or affirmation, and particularly describing the place to be searched, and the persons or things to be seized.

Amendment V

No person shall be held to answer for a capital, or otherwise infamous crime, unless on a presentment or indictment of a Grand Jury, except in cases arising in the land or naval forces, or in the Militia, when in actual service in time of War or public danger; nor

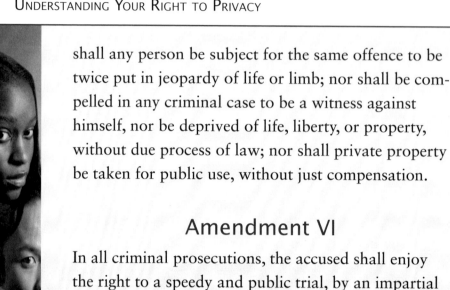

shall any person be subject for the same offence to be twice put in jeopardy of life or limb; nor shall be compelled in any criminal case to be a witness against himself, nor be deprived of life, liberty, or property, without due process of law; nor shall private property be taken for public use, without just compensation.

Amendment VI

In all criminal prosecutions, the accused shall enjoy the right to a speedy and public trial, by an impartial jury of the State and district wherein the crime shall have been committed, which district shall have been previously ascertained by law, and to be informed of the nature and cause of the accusation; to be confronted with the witnesses against him; to have compulsory process for obtaining witnesses in his favor, and to have the Assistance of Counsel for his defense.

Amendment VII

In Suits at common law, where the value in controversy shall exceed twenty dollars, the right of trial by jury shall be preserved, and no fact tried by a jury, shall be otherwise reexamined in any Court of the United States, than according to the rules of the common law.

Amendment VIII

Excessive bail shall not be required, nor excessive fines imposed, nor cruel and unusual punishments inflicted.

Amendment IX

The enumeration in the Constitution, of certain rights, shall not be construed to deny or disparage others retained by the people.

Amendment X

The powers not delegated to the United States by the Constitution, nor prohibited by it to the States, are reserved to the States respectively, or to the people.

abortion The deliberate ending of a pregnancy.

amendment A change or addition made to a legal document.

appeal A request for a higher court to reconsider the ruling of a lower court.

balancing test The act of the Supreme Court weighing constitutional values against each other and deciding to balance different interests or rights.

Bill of Rights The first ten amendments to the U.S. Constitution.

blood spot A blood sample.

COINTELPRO An FBI program that stands for "counterintelligence program" and operated from 1956 to 1971. It was used against many political and civil rights groups as an illegal undercover operation to spy on, infiltrate, and disrupt these organizations.

common law The oldest source of law in the United States that was inherited from Great Britain. Common law is the law of precedent, which means that judges follow decisions in cases that came before. It changes slowly when judges decide that the old rules are obsolete.

curfew law A law that restricts the ability of people to leave their homes, usually during nighttime hours.

due process clause The clause in the Fourteenth Amendment to the Constitution that says no state shall "deprive any person of life, liberty or property, without due process of law." The Fifth Amendment also says that the federal government cannot deny due process.

encryption Making something private by converting it into a code. Software that uses encryption is commonly used for Internet messages.

fundamental rights Rights that are important, but not mentioned in the Constitution. They include the right to marry, have an abortion, and obtain contraception.

grandfather clauses Clauses exempting certain classes of people from the requirements of a piece of legislation affecting their previous rights, privileges, or practices.

in re A term that is often used in place of "ex parte," which means a judicial proceeding by or for one party without contest by an adverse party. A typical ex parte proceeding may be one brought by a prisoner seeking a writ of habeas corpus (a court order directing an official who has a person in custody to bring the prisoner to court and to show cause for that person's detention).

originalist A person who believes that in interpreting the Constitution, one looks to the practices and beliefs of the people who wrote the Constitution.

parental consent law A law that requires a parent's permission for minors who live at home.

precedent A model or example that may be followed or referred to later.

probable cause Cause to suspect the commission of a crime.

prosecute To carry out legal action against a person who has been accused of an offense.

surveillance The act of watching and monitoring the activities of someone.

textualism The idea that there can be no rights in the Constitution that are not specifically written down.

American Civil Liberties Union (ACLU)

125 Broad Street, 18 Floor

New York, NY 10004

(212) 549-2500

Web site: http://www.aclu.org

This national organization protects privacy rights and has state and local chapters.

Center for Constitutional Rights

666 Broadway, 7 Floor

New York, NY 10012

(212) 614-6464

Web site: http://www.ccrjustice.org

The Center for Constitutional Rights is a nonprofit educational and legal organization dedicated to protecting civil rights.

CyberAngels

P.O. Box 3171

Allentown, PA 18106

Web site: http://www.cyberangels.org

This organization provides Internet safety information to schools and families and works to stop computer fraud.

Electronic Privacy Information Center (EPIC)

1718 Connecticut Avenue NW, Suite 200

Washington, DC 20009

(202) 483-1140

Web site: http://www.epic.org

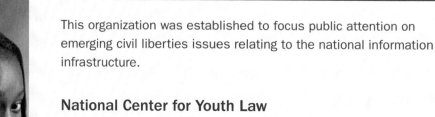

This organization was established to focus public attention on emerging civil liberties issues relating to the national information infrastructure.

National Center for Youth Law

405 Fourteenth Street, 15 Floor

Oakland, CA 94612-2701

(510) 835-8098

Web site: http://www.youthlaw.org

This private, nonprofit law office serves the legal needs of children and their families and runs the Web site TeenHealthRights.org.

NetSmartz

Charles B. Wang International

699 Prince Street

Alexandria, VA 22314-3175

(800) 843-5678

Web site: http://www.netsmartz.org

This organization, sponsored by the National Center for Missing & Exploited Children and Boys & Girls Clubs of America, teaches teens and children how to stay safe and protect their privacy on the Internet.

Privacy International

666 Pennsylvania Avenue SE, Suite 301

Washington, DC 20003

(202) 544-9240

Web site: http://www.privacyinternational.org

This human rights group was formed in 1990 as a watchdog on surveillance by governments and corporations. It is based in London and has an office in Washington, D.C.

U.S. Department of Justice
Civil Rights Division
950 Pennsylvania Avenue SW
Washington, DC 20530
Web site: http://www.justice.gov/crt
The Civil Rights Division of the U.S. Department of Justice works to uphold the civil and constitutional rights of everyone, especially those who are the most vulnerable in U.S. society.

Web Sites

Due to the changing nature of Internet links, Rosen Publishing has developed an online list of Web sites related to the subject of this book. This site is updated regularly. Please use this link to access the list:

http://www.rosenlinks.com/pfcd/priv

Bridegam, Martha. *Search and Seizure*. Philadelphia, PA: Chelsea House, 2005.

Dougherty, Terri. *Freedom of Expression and the Internet* (Hot Topics). Farmington Hills, MI: Lucent Books, 2010.

Espejo, Roman. *Privacy* (Opposing Viewpoints). Farmington Hills, MI: Greenhaven Press, 2010.

Fridell, Ron. *Privacy vs. Security: Your Rights in Conflict* (Issues in Focus). Berkeley Heights, NJ: Enslow Publishers, 2004.

Harding, Lauri. *DNA Databases* (At Issue Series). Farmington Hills, MI: Greenhaven, 2007.

Henderson, Harry. *Privacy in the Information Age* (Library in a Book). New York, NY: Facts On File, 2006.

Hudson, David L., Jr. *Open Government: An American Tradition Faces National Security, Privacy, and Other Challenges* (Point Counterpoint). New York, NY: Chelsea House, 2005.

Hudson, David L., Jr. *The Right to Privacy* (Point Counterpoint). New York, NY: Chelsea House, 2009.

Kallen, Stuart A. *Are Privacy Rights Being Violated?* Farmington Hills, MI: Greenhaven, 2005.

Kuhn, Betsy. *Prying Eyes: Privacy in the Twenty-First Century*. Minneapolis, MN: Twenty-First Century Books, 2008.

Marcovitz, Harold. *Privacy Rights and the PATRIOT Act*. Edina, MN: ABDO Publishing, 2008.

Morris, Neil. *Do We Have a Right to Privacy?* (What Do You Think?). Portsmouth, NH: Heinemann, 2007.

Smith, Rich. *Fourth Amendment: The Right to Privacy*. Edina, MN: ABDO Publishing, 2008.

Stefoff, Rebecca. *Security v. Privacy* (Open for Debate). Salt Lake City, UT: Benchmark Books, 2007.

Taylor-Butler, Christine. *The Bill of Rights*. New York, NY: Children's Press, 2008.

Tubb, Kristin O'Donnell. *Freedom from Unfair Searches and Seizures* (Bill of Rights). Farmington Hills, MI: Greenhaven Press, 2005.

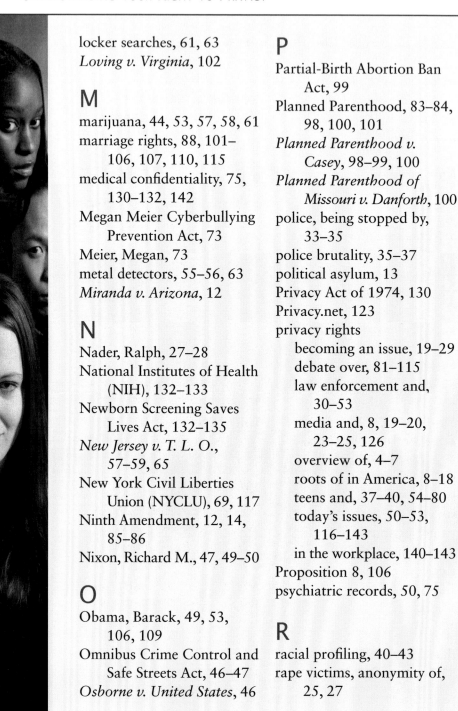

About the Authors

Kathy Furgang is a writer and editor in the education market who has written books on subjects as diverse as the Seventh Amendment and Ninth Amendment, the environment, and the economy. She writes for students of all ages.

Frank Gatta earned a B.A. in philosophy and worked as an advocate for homeless people in New York before earning his law degree. He lives in Virginia.

Photo Credits